I0833195

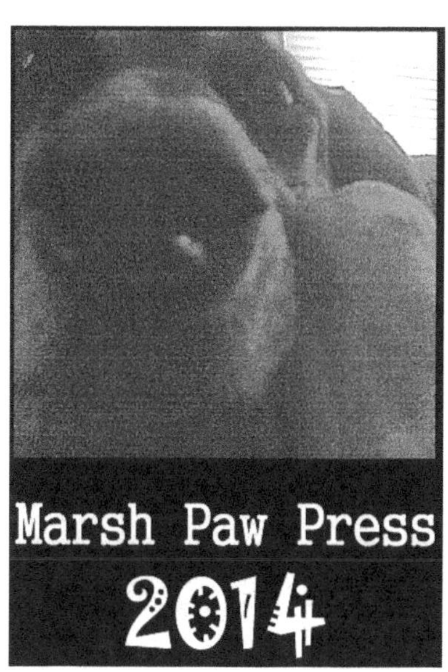
Marsh Paw Press
2014

Other books by Eric C. Harrison

Denizens of Distraction

Art collection # 2

$#&%!!!

Art collection # 3

Picture Of A Paranoid

Poems, Prose & Short Stories, 2002-2012

At The Bottom Of The Big Top

A horror story told with poems.

Finding The Secret Sea

An experiment in spontaneity of image/word association

Art by Eric C. Harrison / words by Mike Maguire

Quirkish Delight

Drawings and Ink-Sketches done in 2012

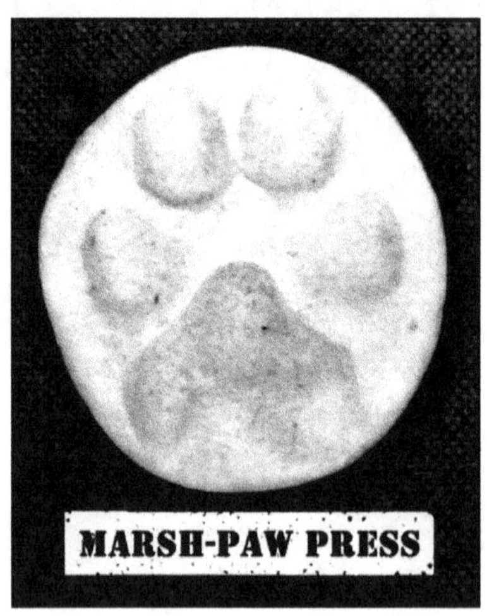

Visit Marsh-Paw Press online

www.marshpawpress.com

www.facebook.com/marshpawpress

BLACKENED WHITE

Art Collection # 1

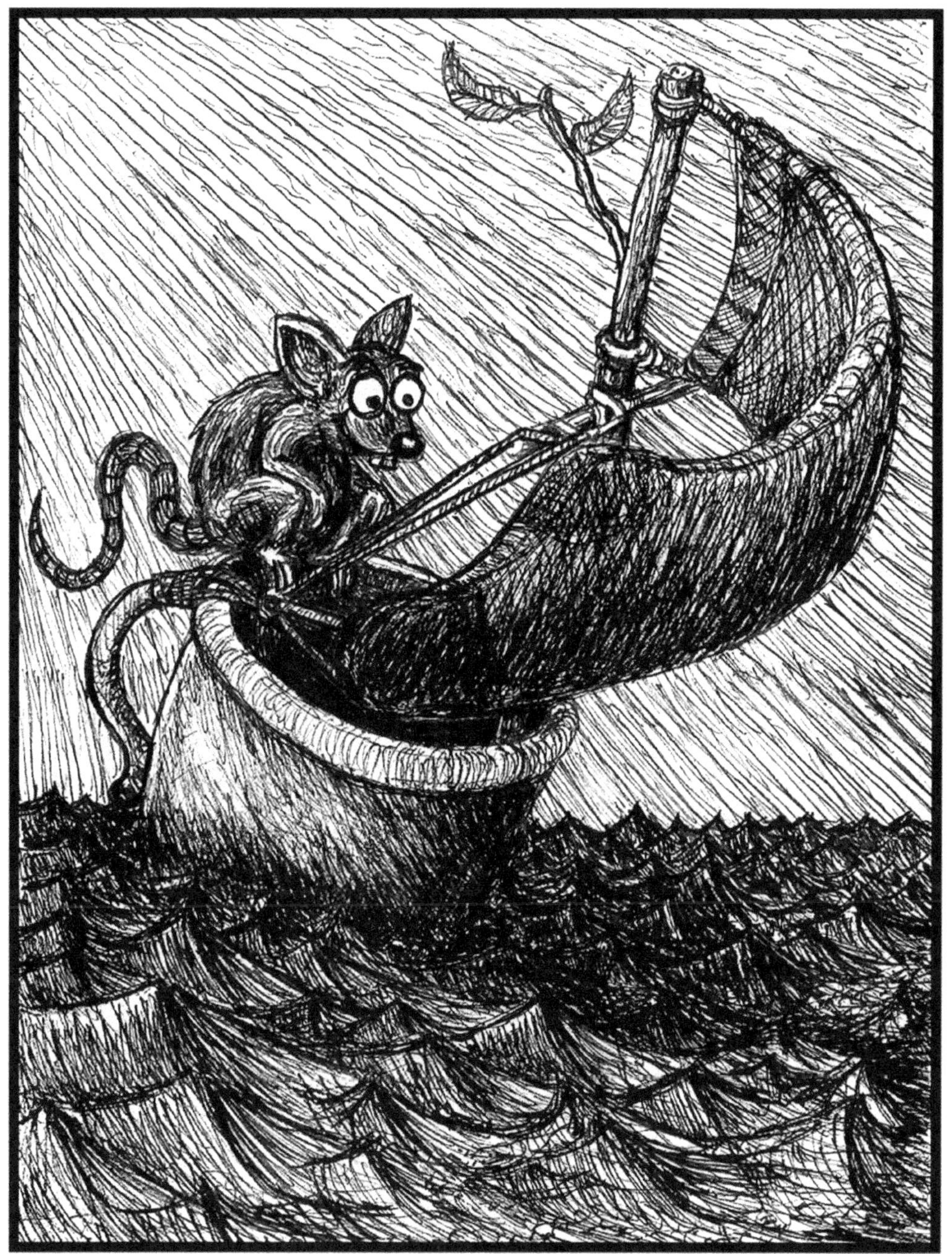

By

Eric C. Harrison

Marsh Paw Press

2012

Blackened White
Art Collection # 1

By Eric C. Harrison
circa 1986-2012

ISBN 978-0-9888040-5-0

Write to Stilldiseased@aol.com

Published by Marsh Paw Press
Saltmarsh, Massachusetts

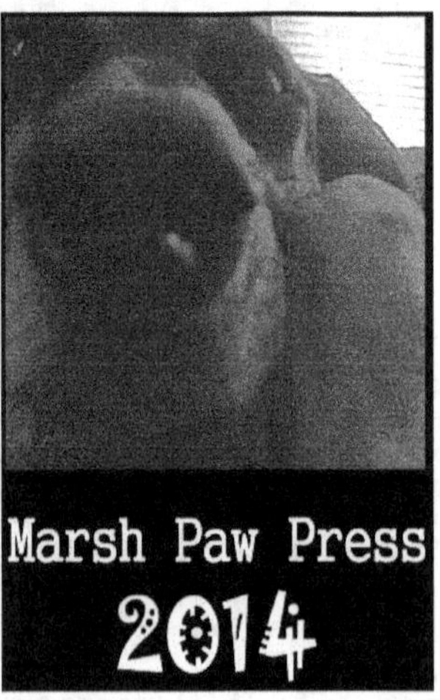

** First Paperback Edition*
June, 2014

Indroduction

In *Blackened White: Art collection # 1-* artist, musician and writer, Eric C. Harrison creates a visual myth, populated by hideous beasts, underpinned by gallows humor, and filled with endlessly suggestive images that both startle and intrigue the viewer. The book is a testament to an artist of remarkable ability who remains true to his vision.

In the past, my experience with Harrison's work has been more with the written word, poems that admittedly flow from his misanthropic, paranoid assessment of the world. In *Blackened White,* which exists somewhere in a kind of swirling vortex where doodling and illustration become fine art, he accomplishes a similar vision. The observer is immediately swept into a domain that harbors one-eyed disembodied hearts, mangled demons, pot smoking dinosaurs, mad scientists, mysterious dark tunnels, sea monsters, flying musical symbols as well as the artist's beloved dogs.

While I don't necessarily feel qualified to comment on artwork or music, like most people, I know what I like, and I know what drives my interest and curiosity.

I have shown Harrison's book to several people to gauge their reactions. One, a novice artist, immediately said, he's just doodling, then paused as he slowly flipped through the pages, and finished by saying, but he's the best damn doodler I've ever seen. Another, a teenager and budding guitarist, and not a fan of art, was fascinated by the churning turmoil in which an eye socket may be a key hole in a door to hell, and a deformed man might walk on crutches and wheels instead of feet.

To put it simply, Harrison's dynamic art work is infused with an energy that will help draw many readers and viewers to his post-industrial horror myth.

Tim Peeler
Editor & Creator of Third Lung Review
Author of Blood River & Checking Out

Note

This is the second release of Blackened White.

The first version was released in 2012 as a deluxe, hardcover photobook. It is a beautiful book but its expense made it unavailable to many people.

This version gives me more freedom in presenting each drawing by giving each one its own page. The more reasonable cost of this form of media also allows me to include additional artwork and present the text at the beginning and the end in a more comfortable, less condensed way.

The titles and information about these drawings has been put together in an index at the back of this book. This information was put out of the way to prevent it from interfering with the initial impression of each viewer.

Eric C. Harrison
April, 2014

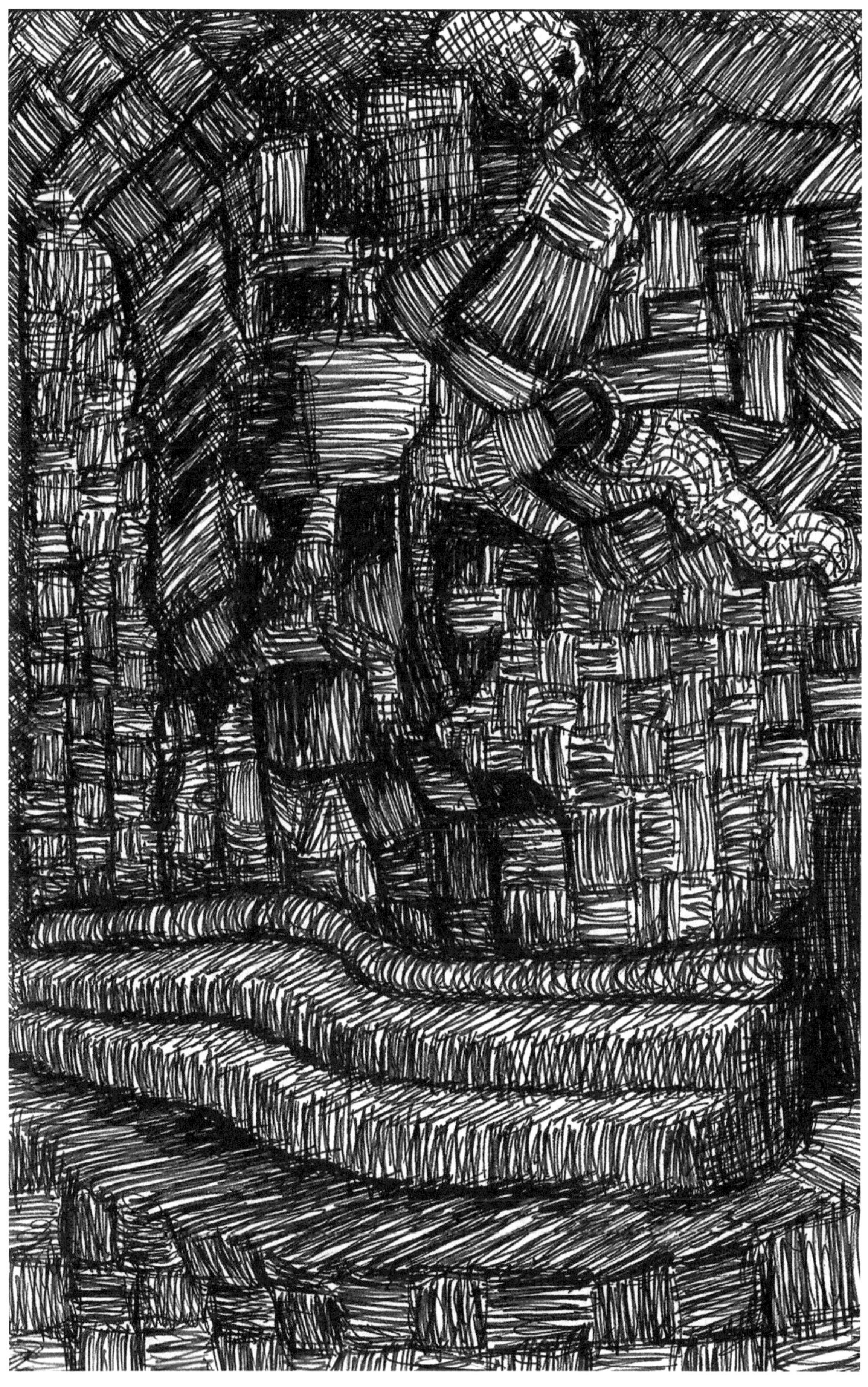

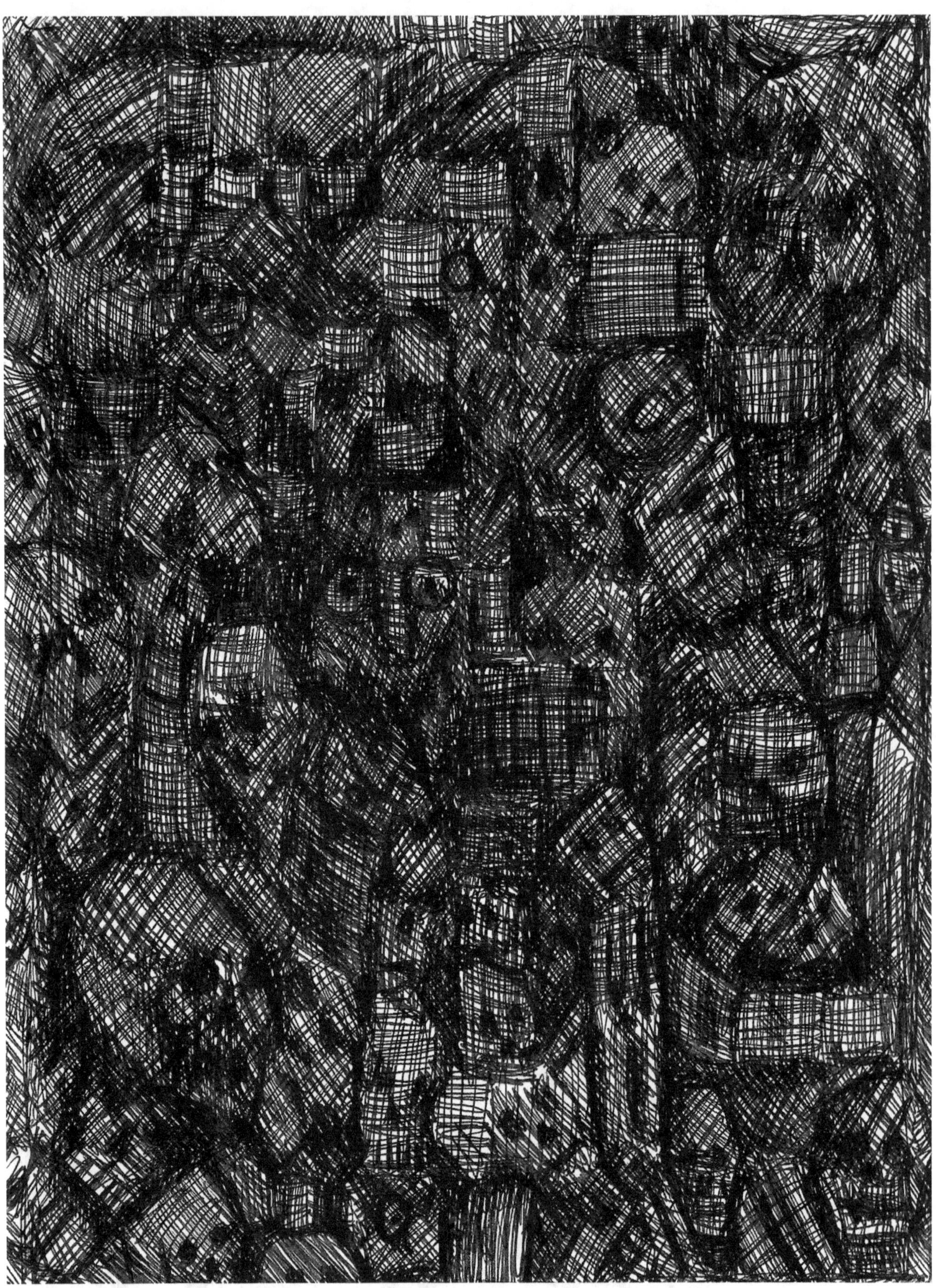

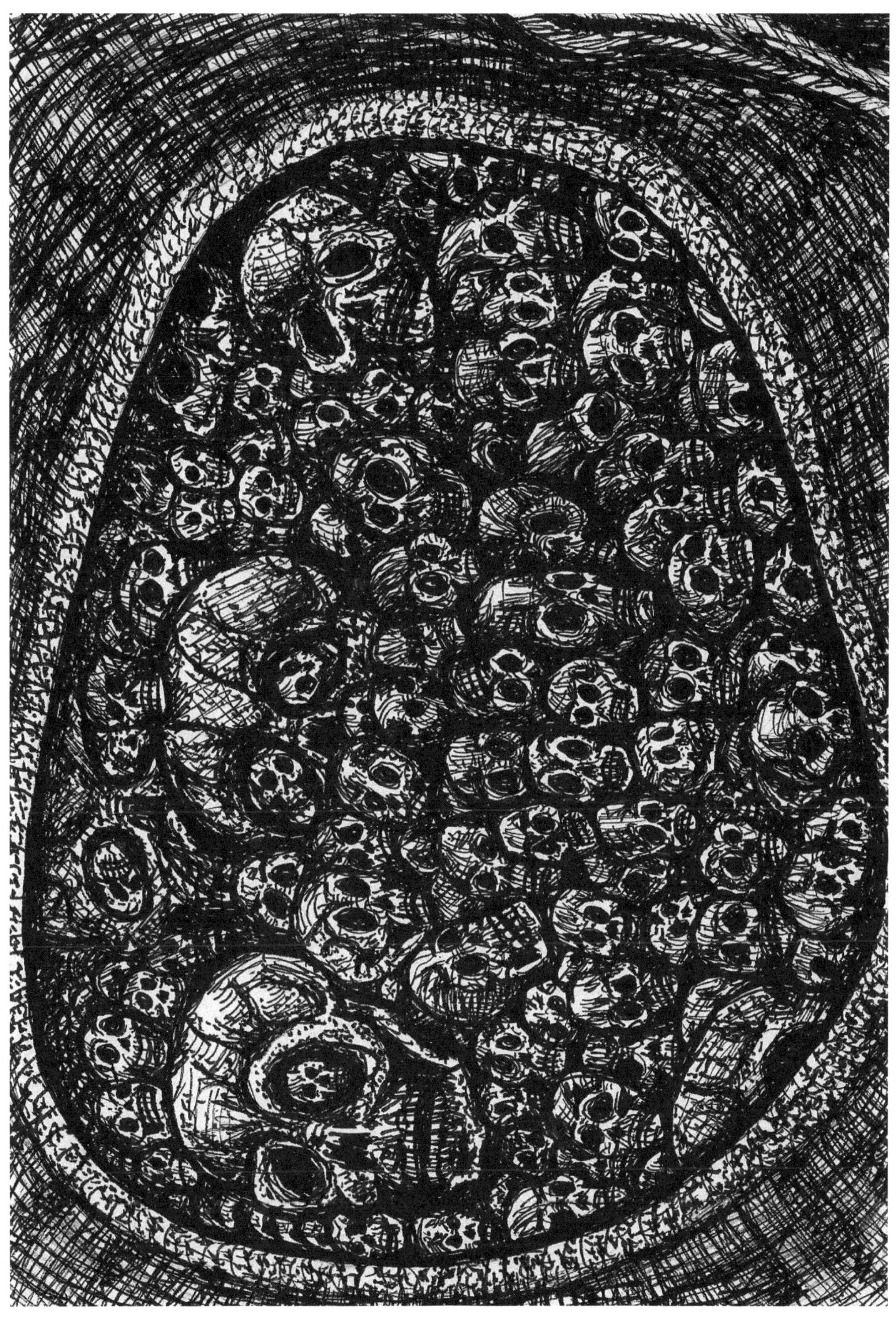

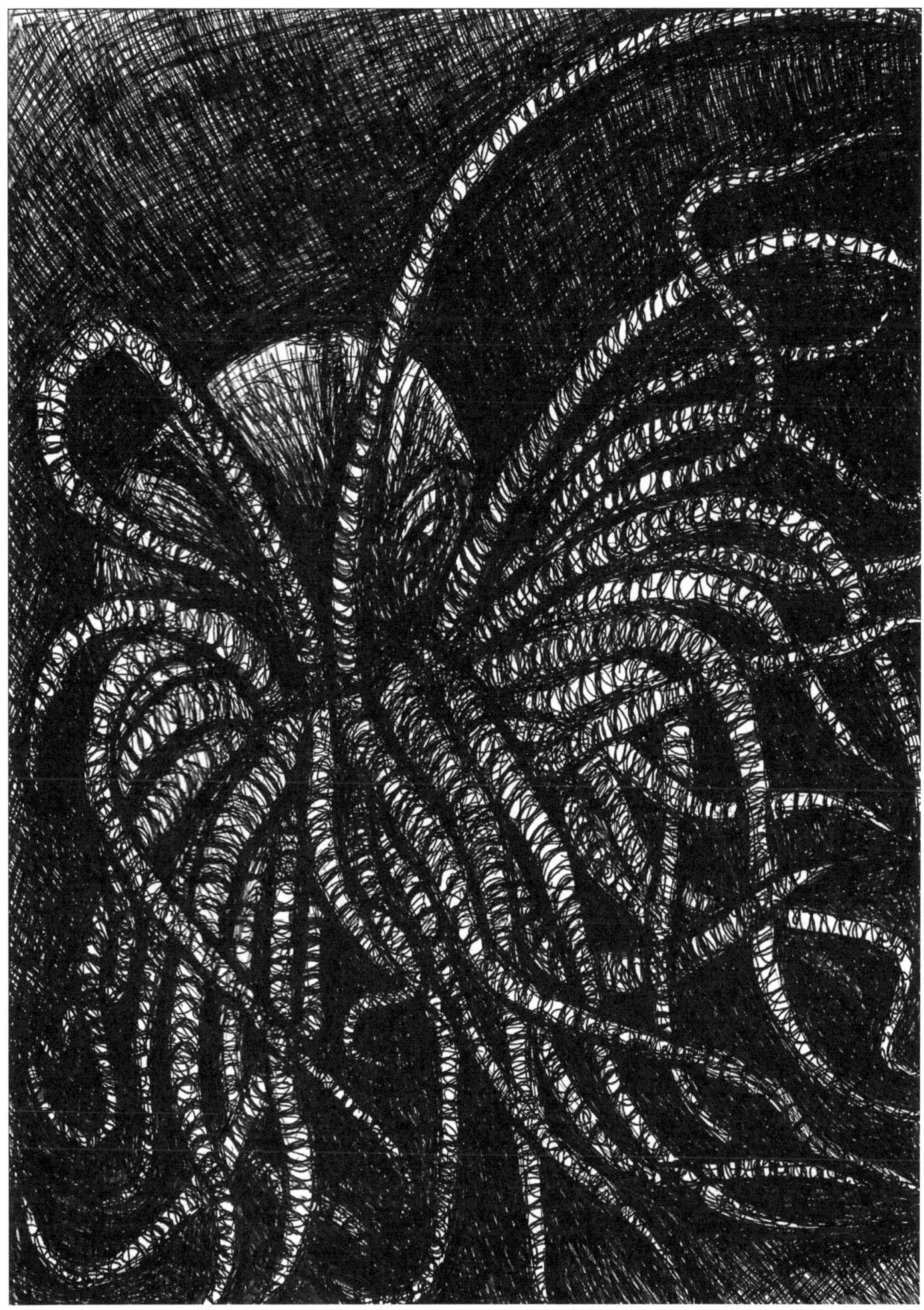

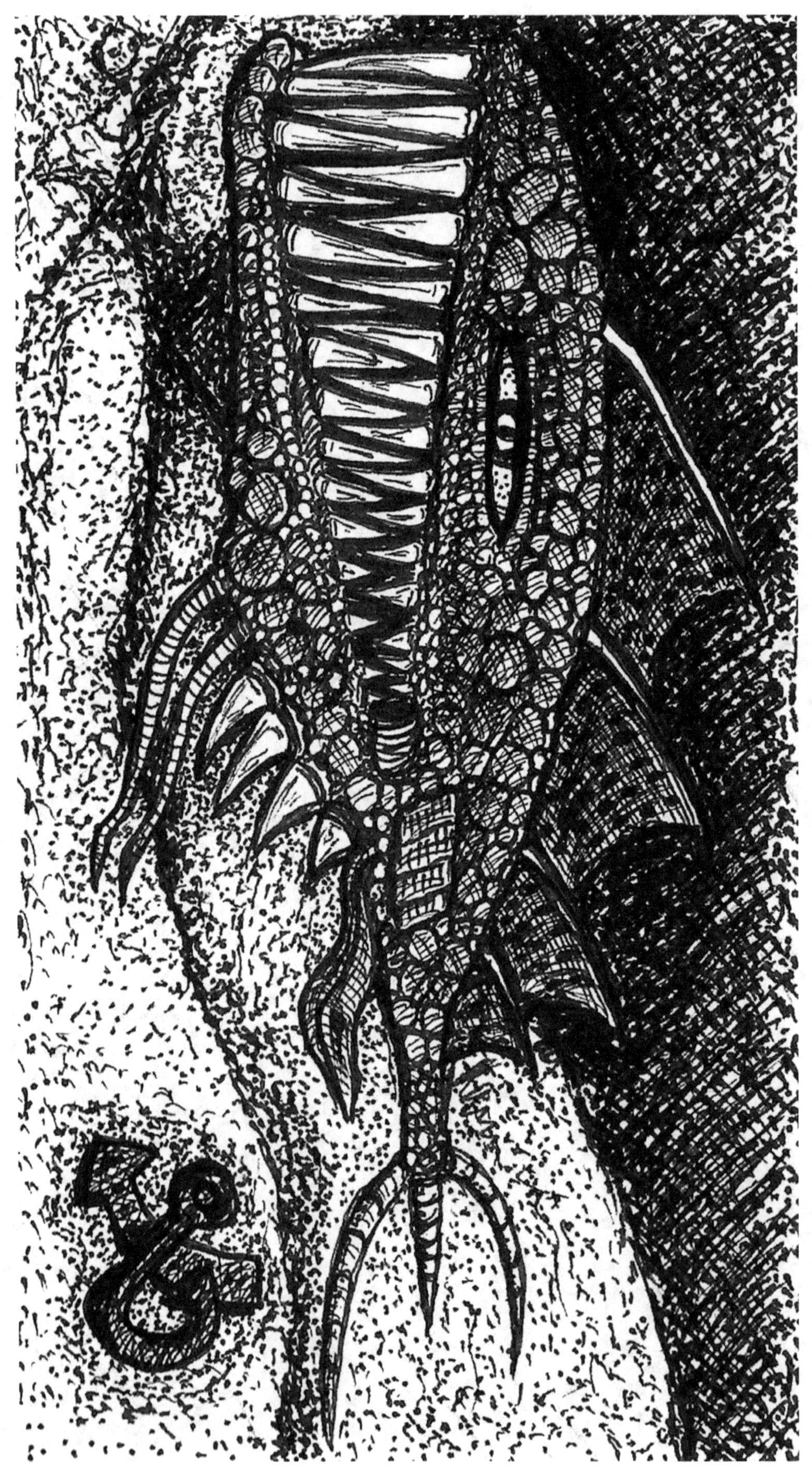

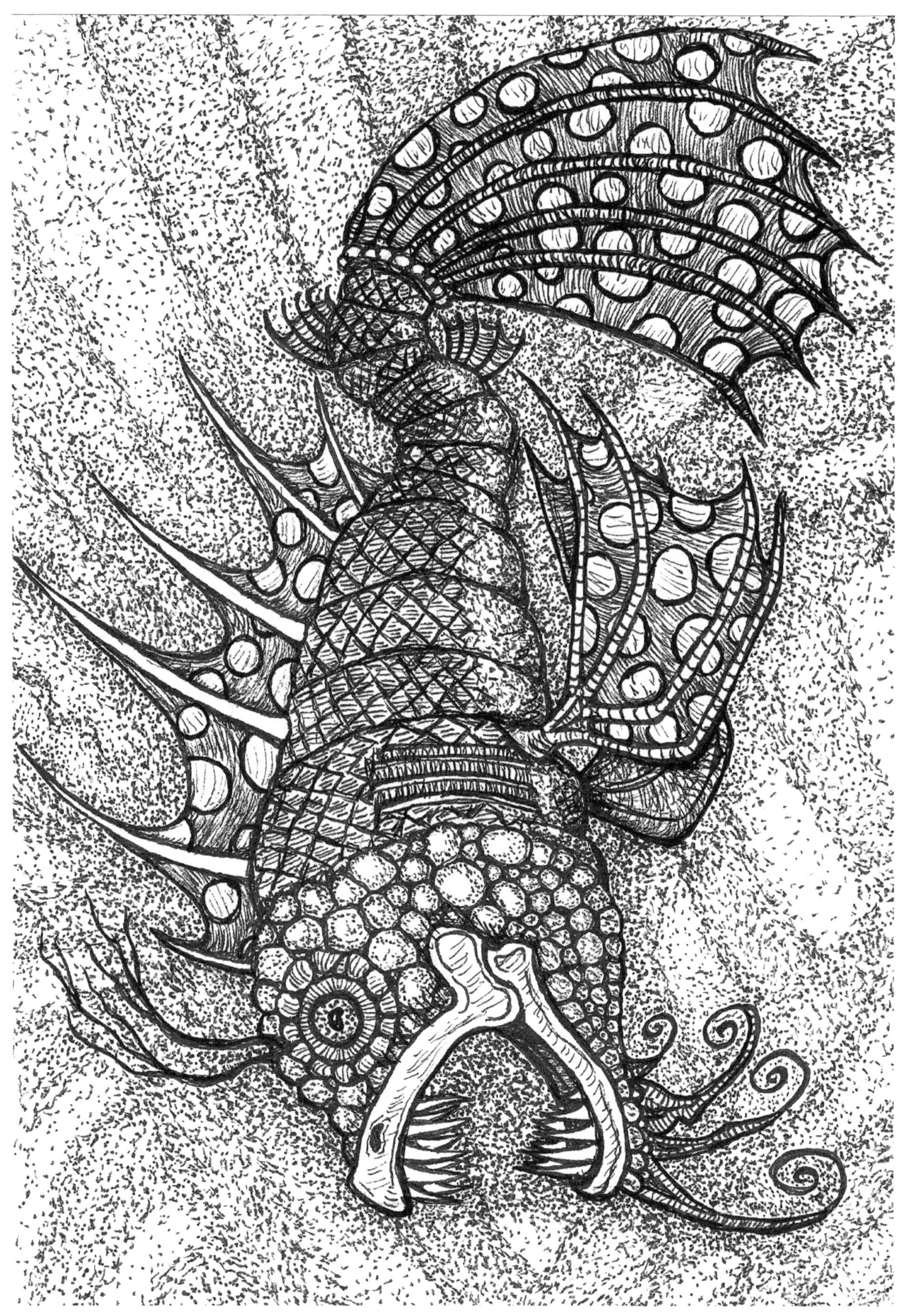

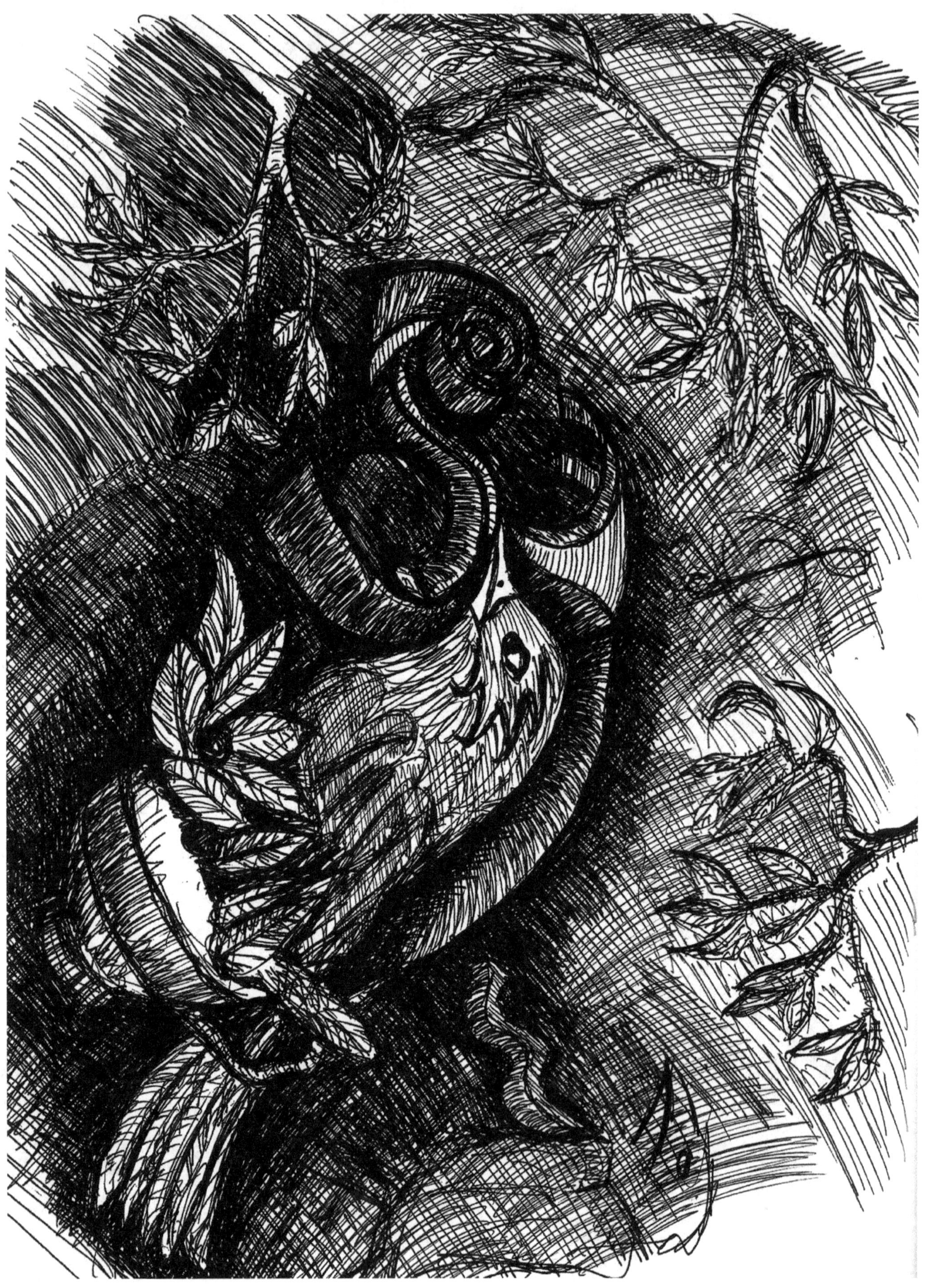

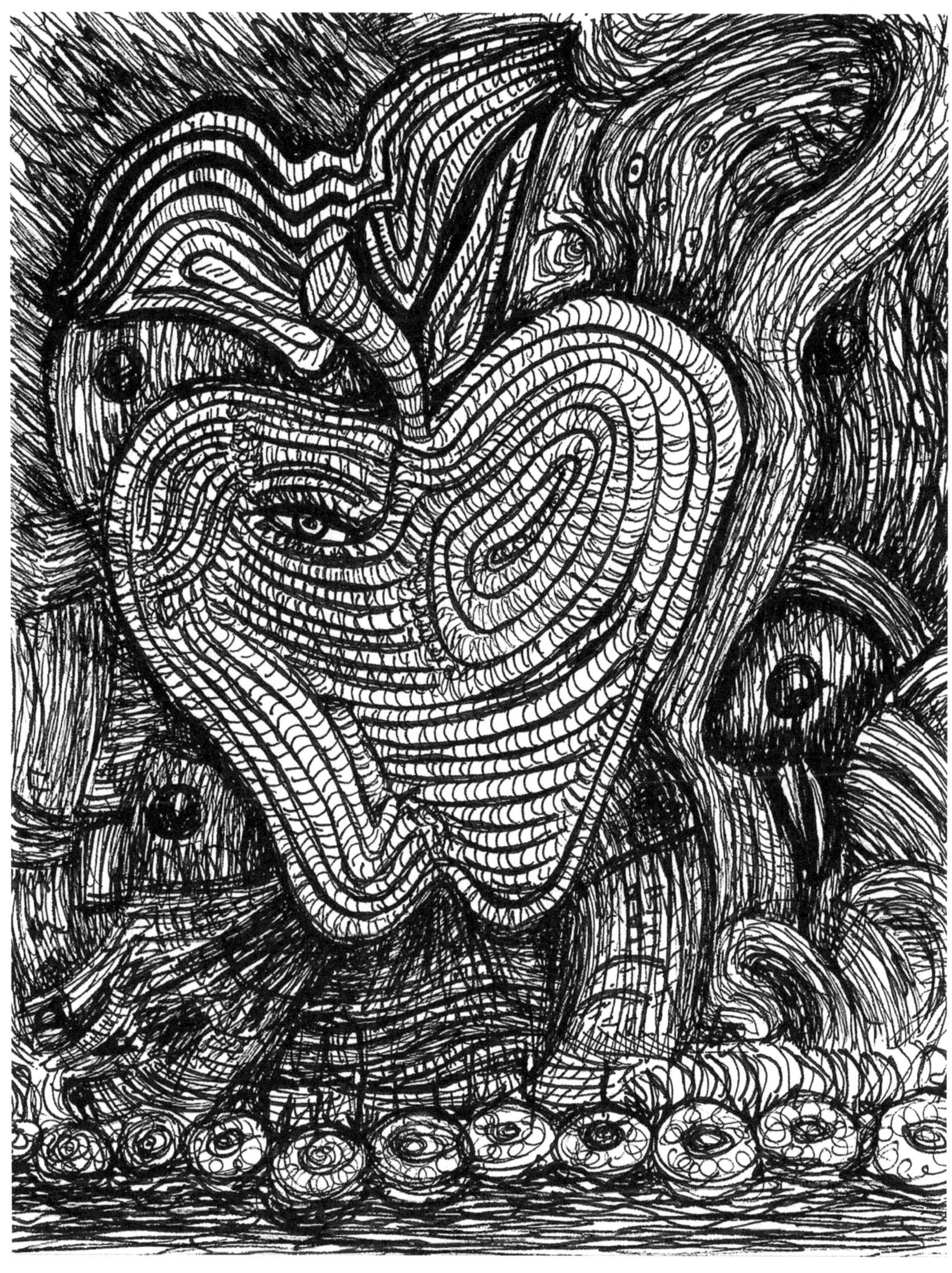

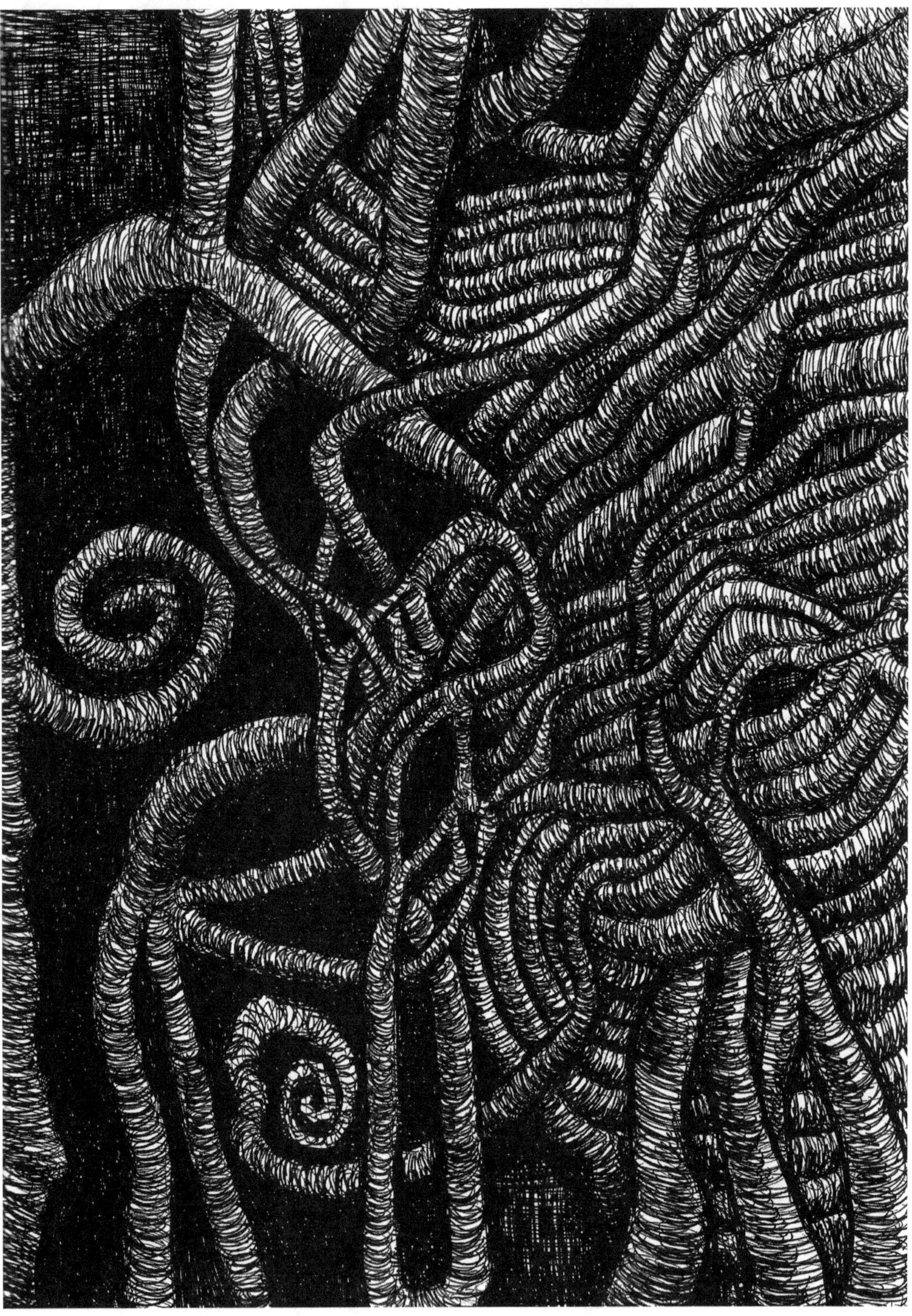

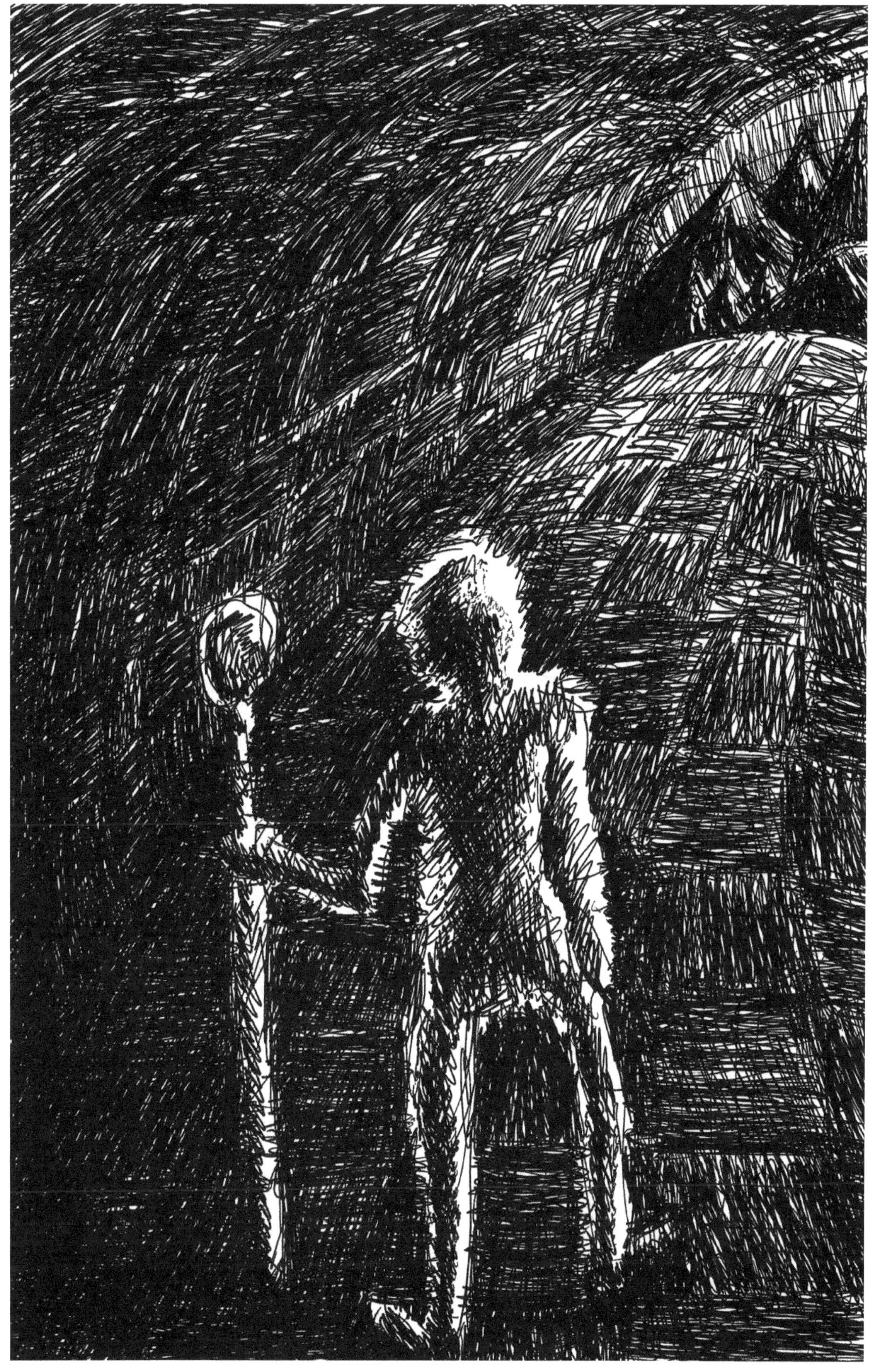

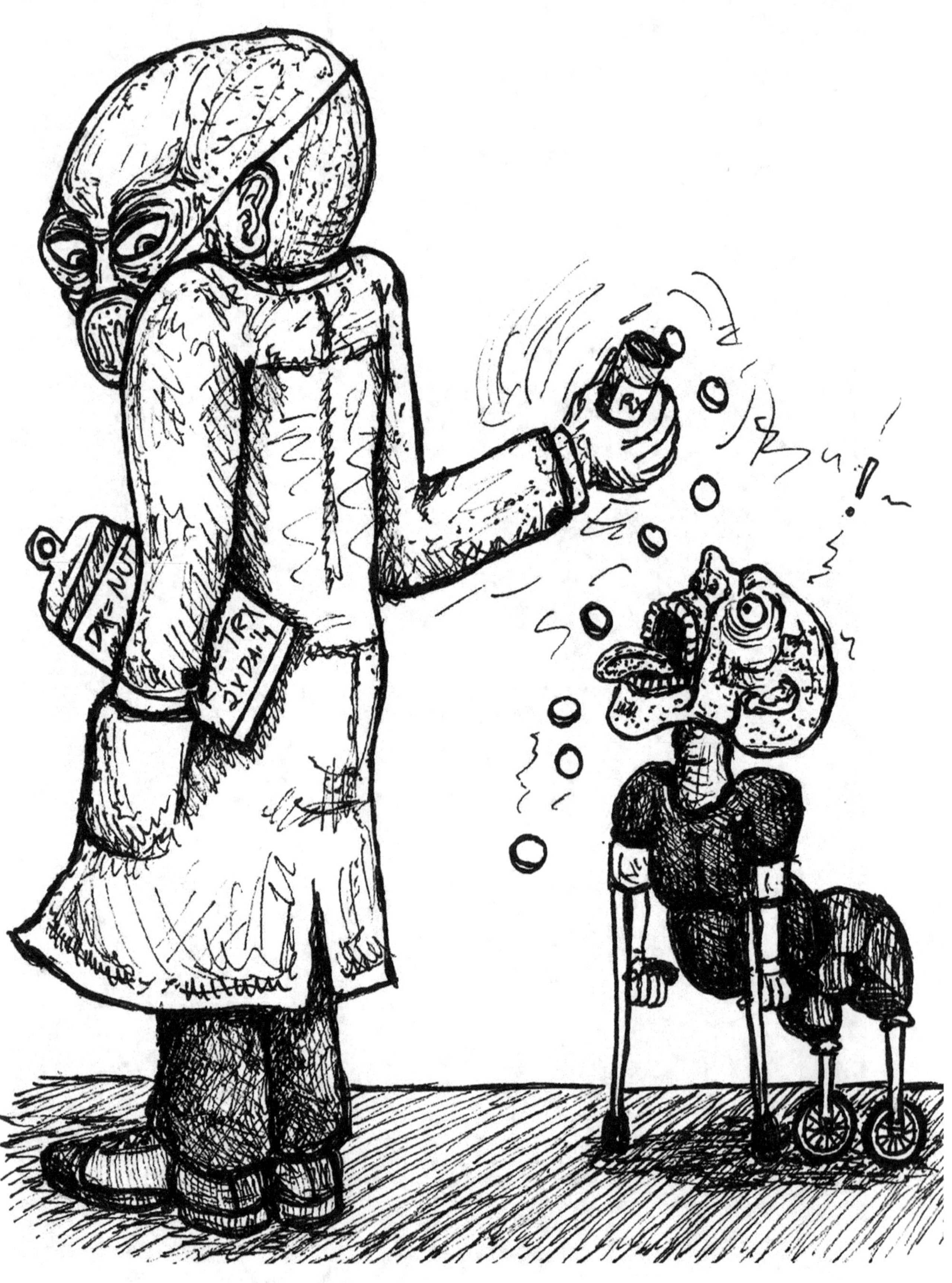
DR=NUT
TRY
RX

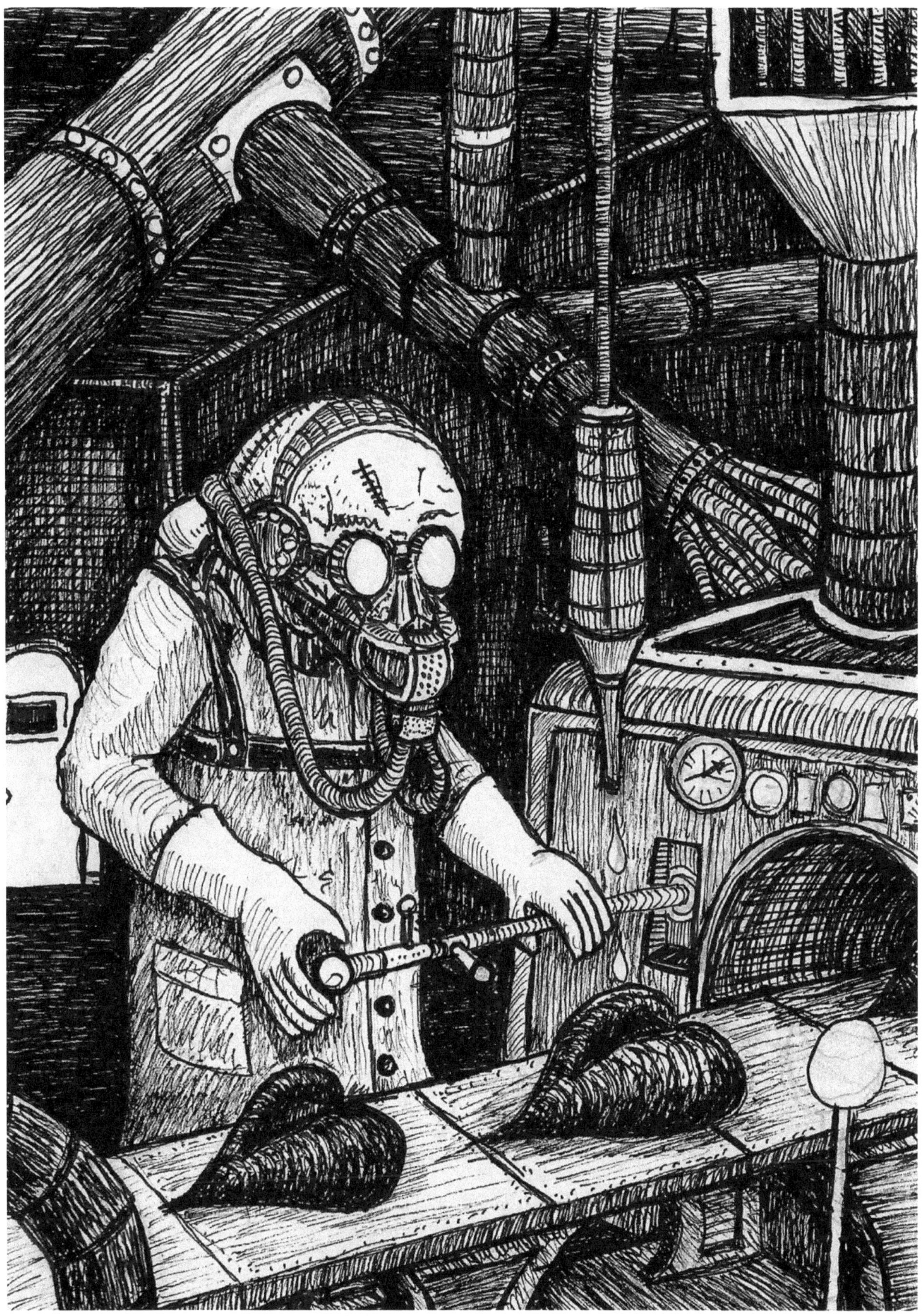

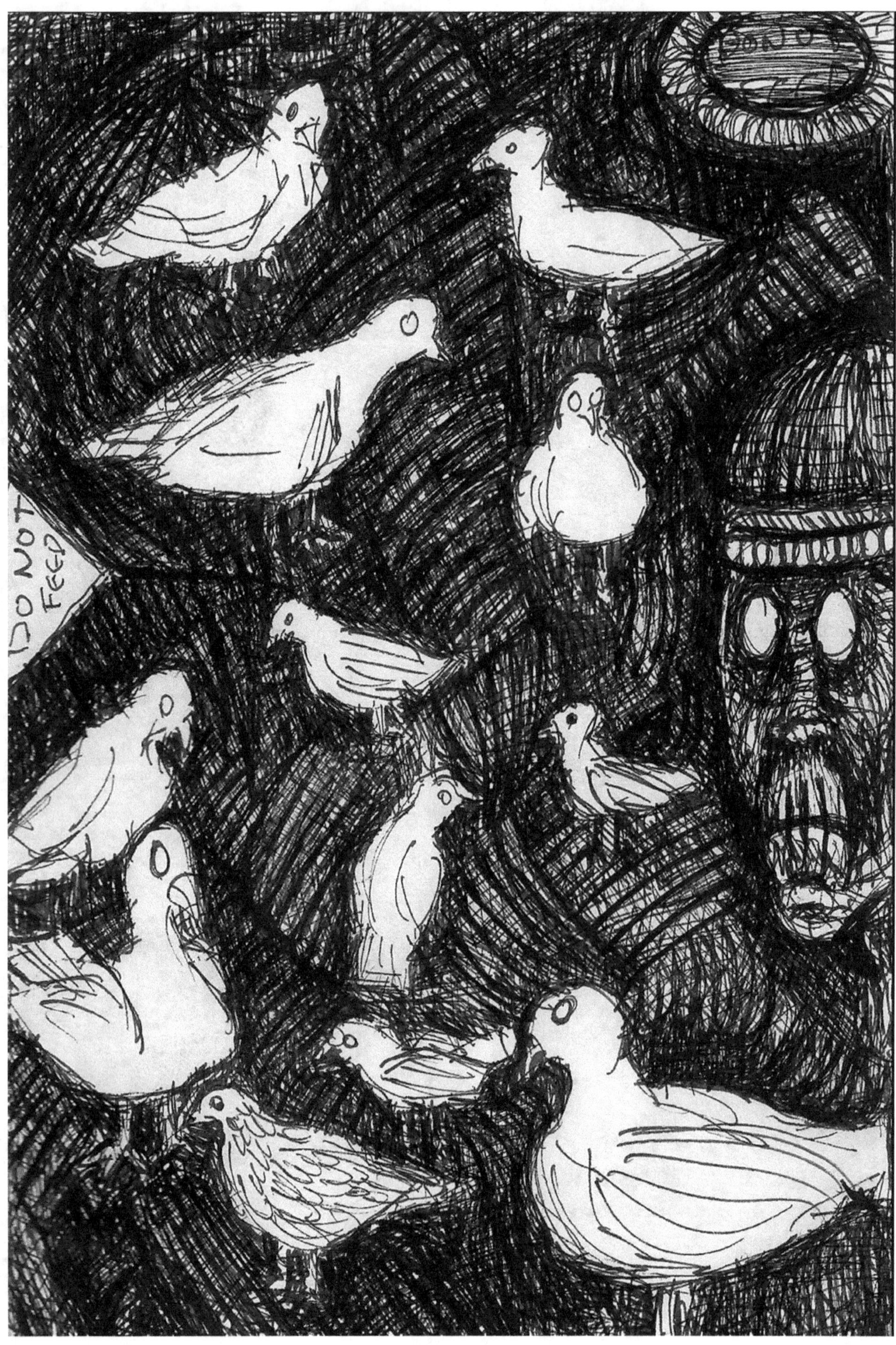
DO NOT FEED

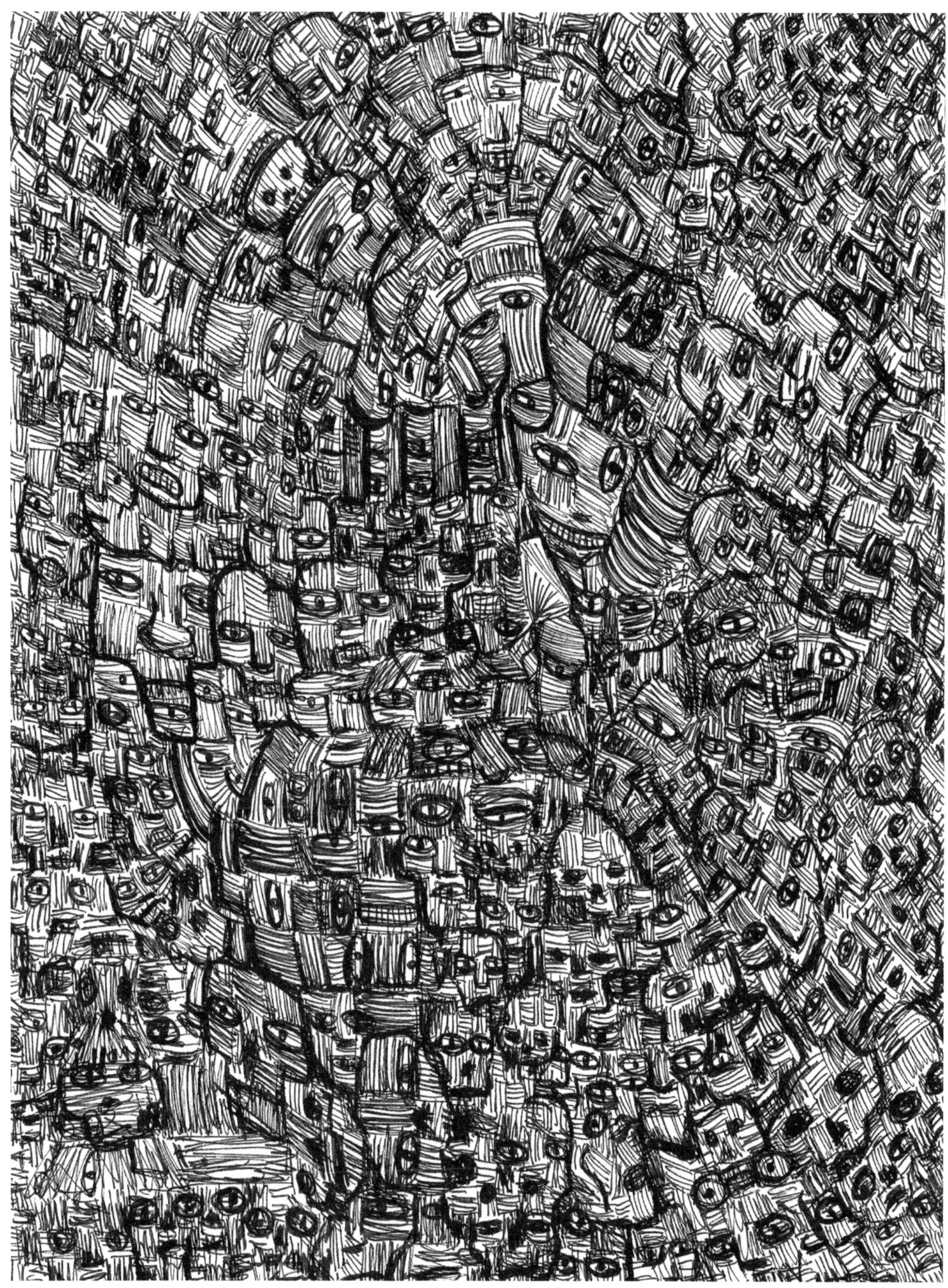

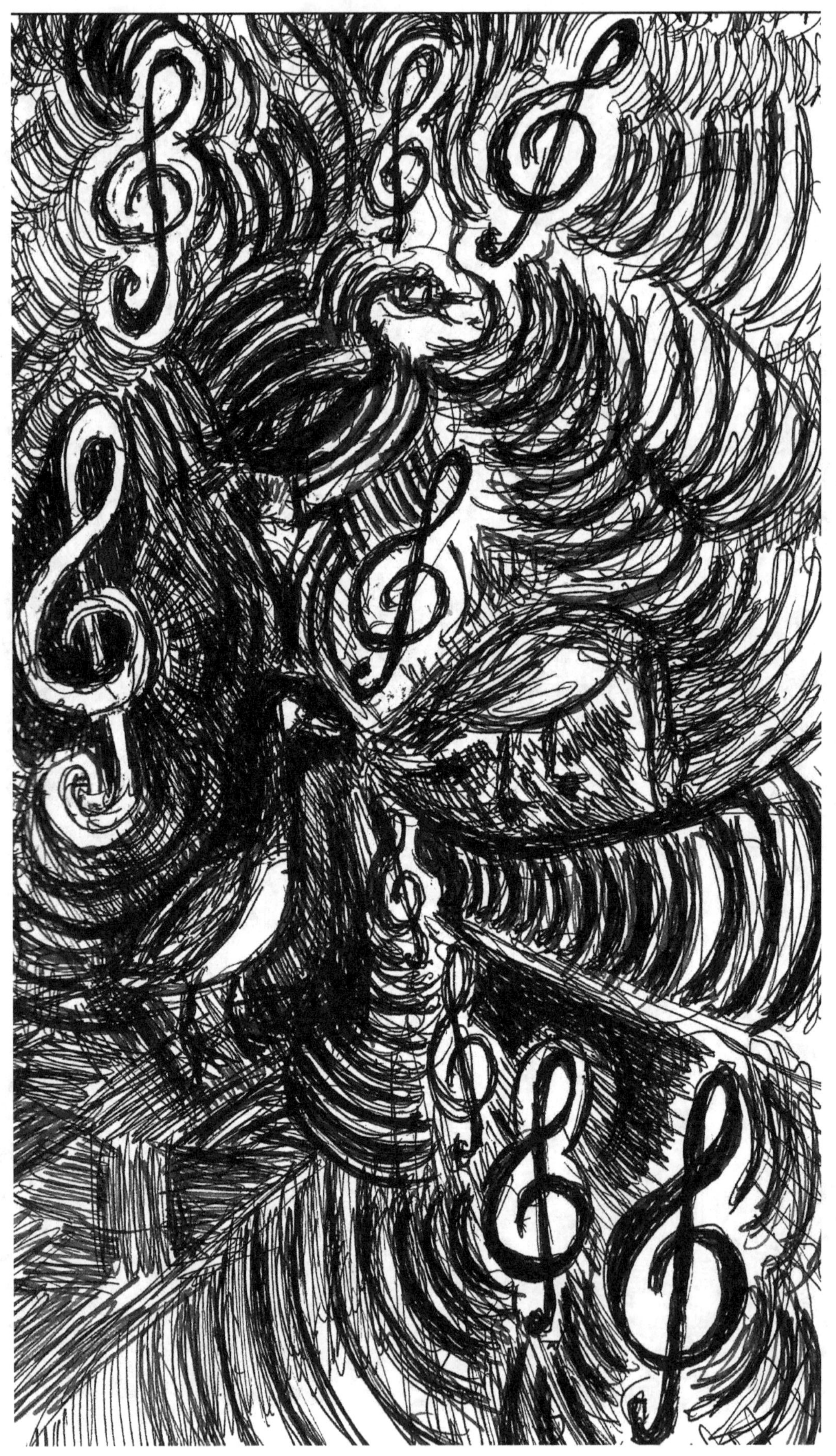

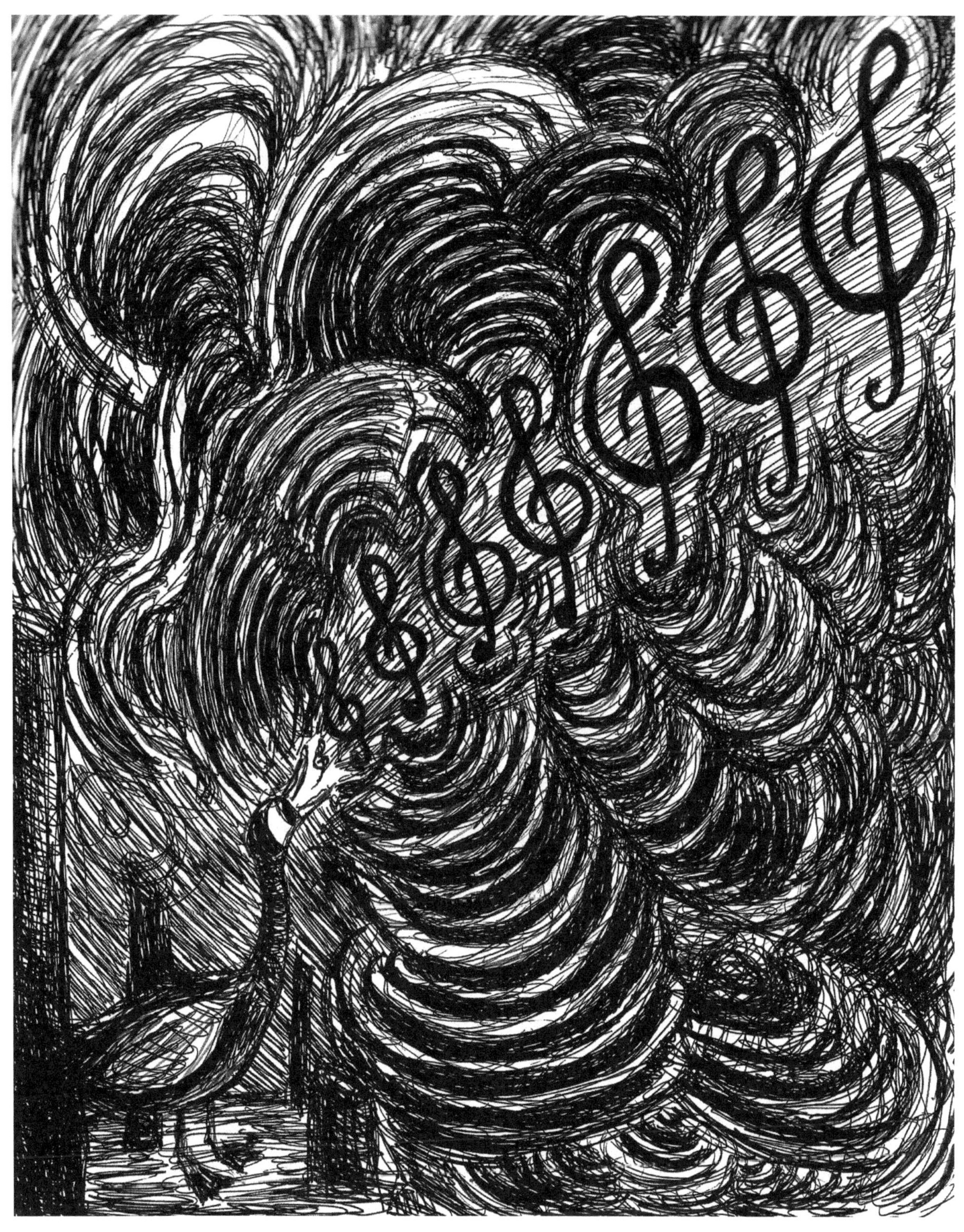

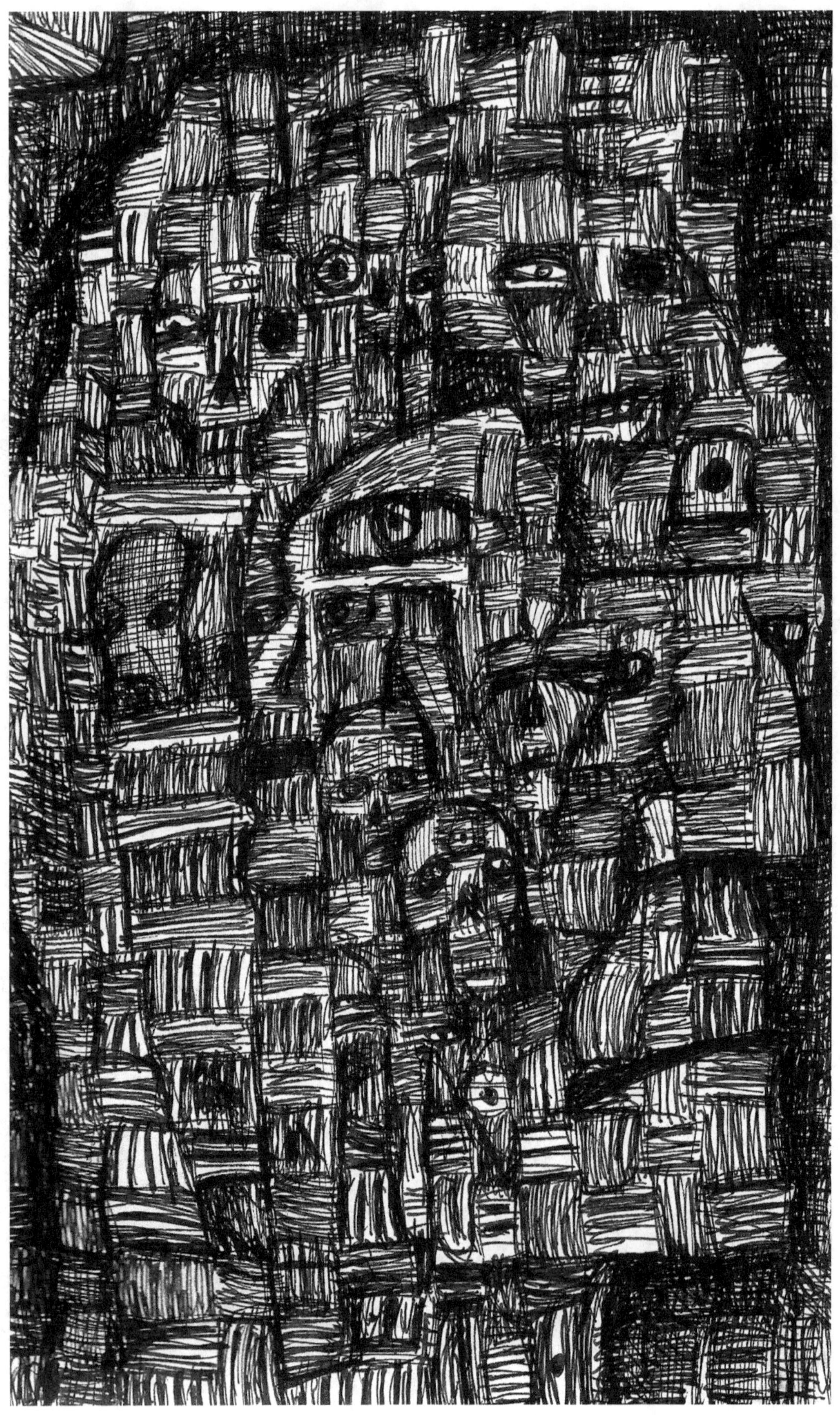

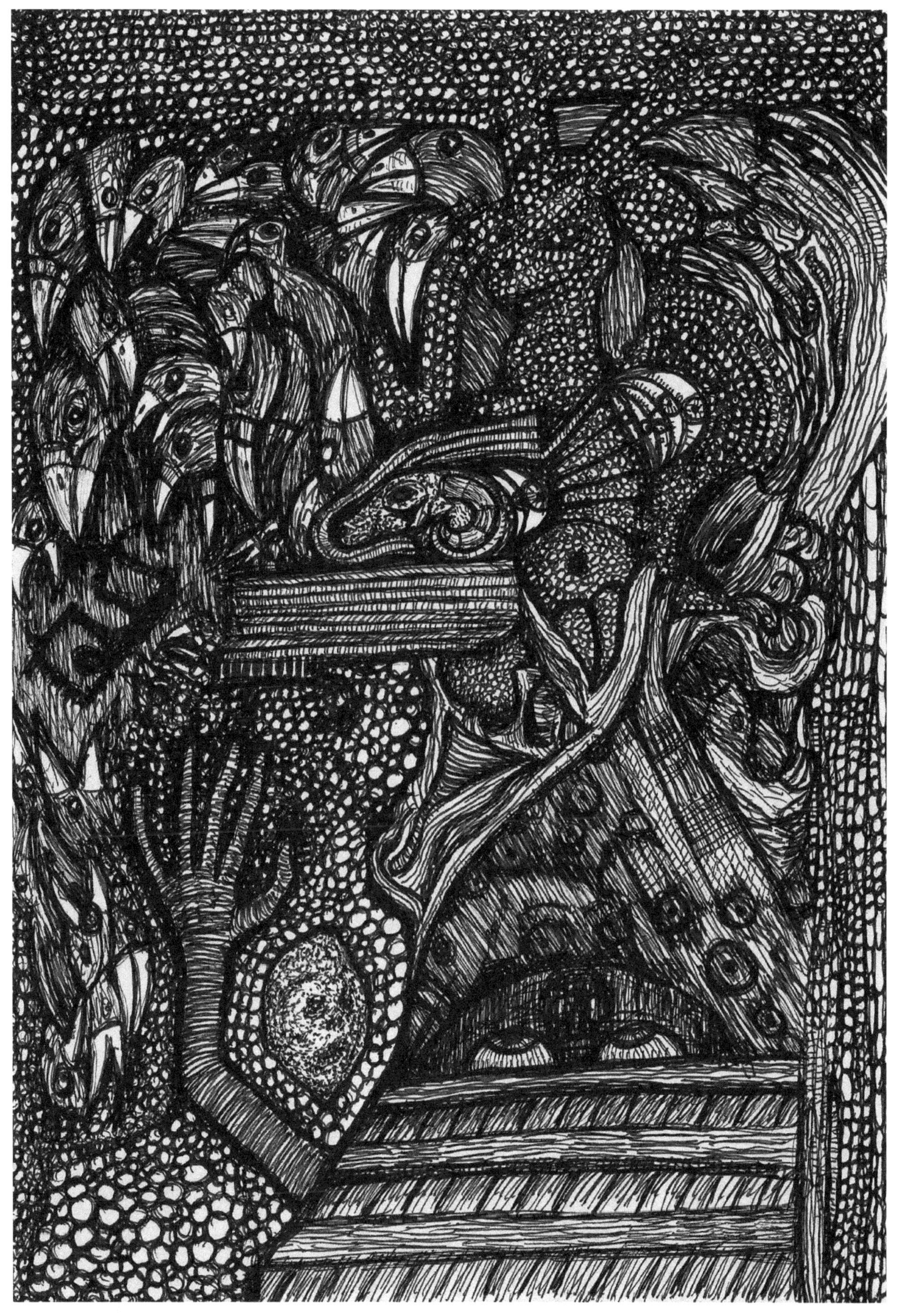

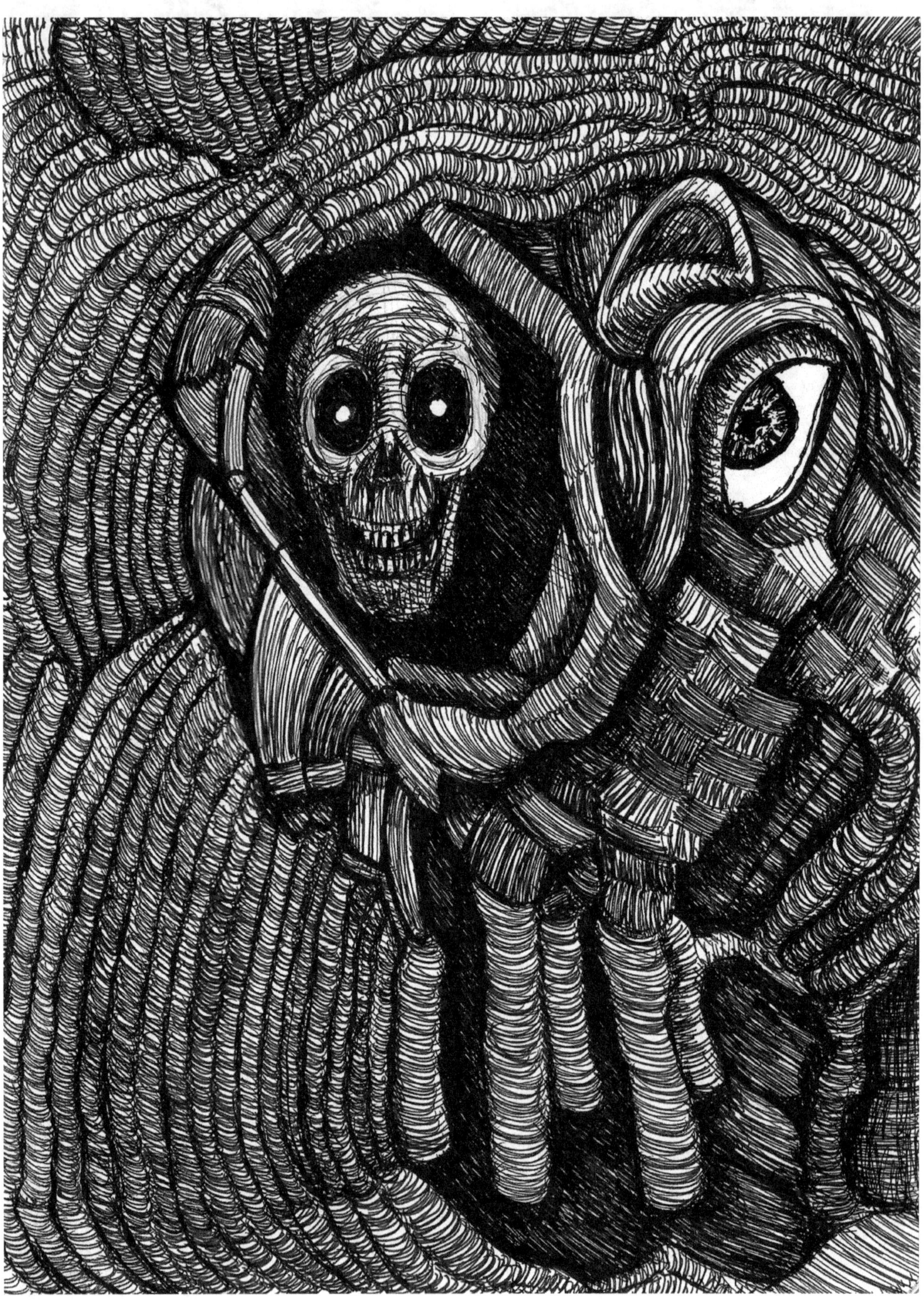

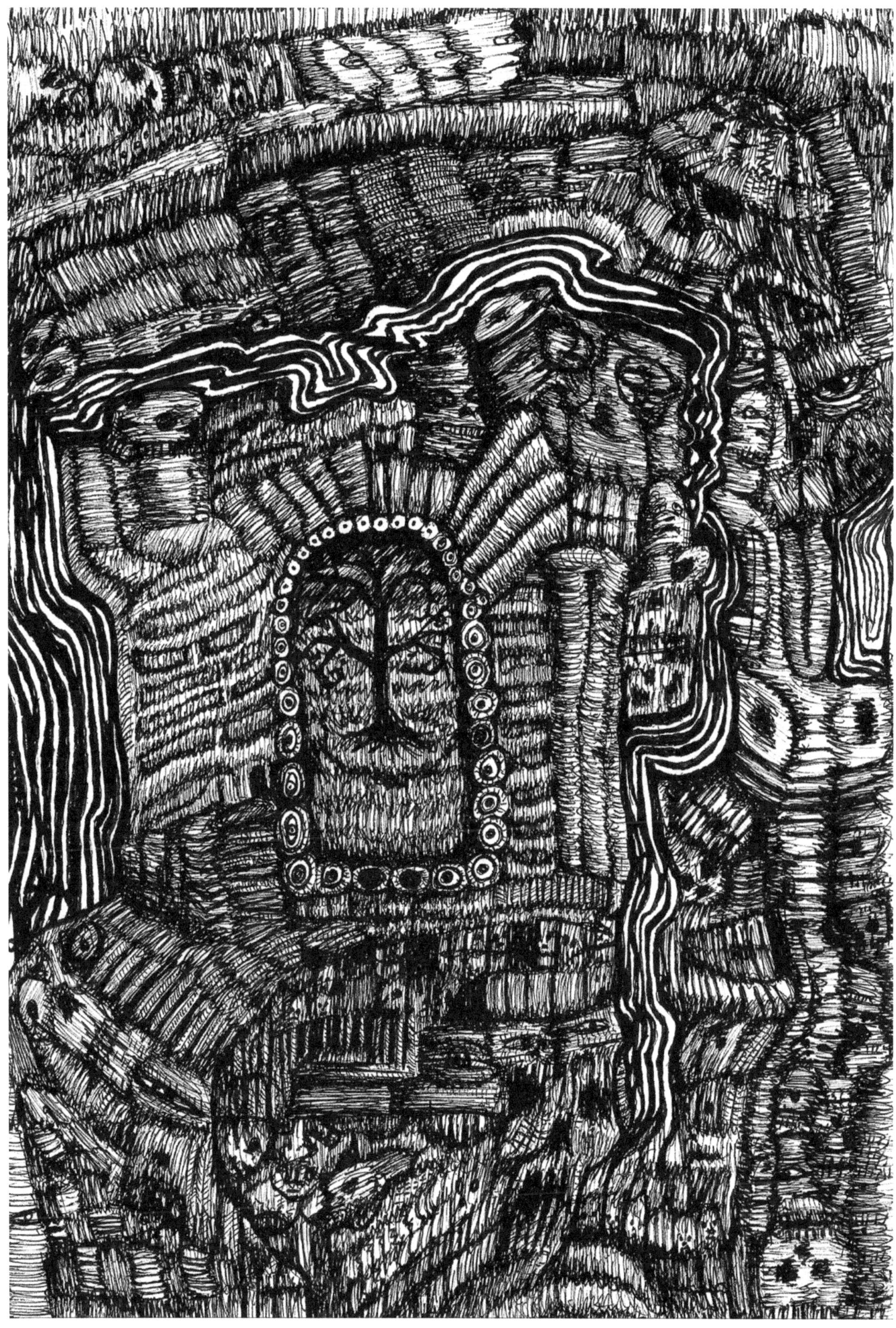

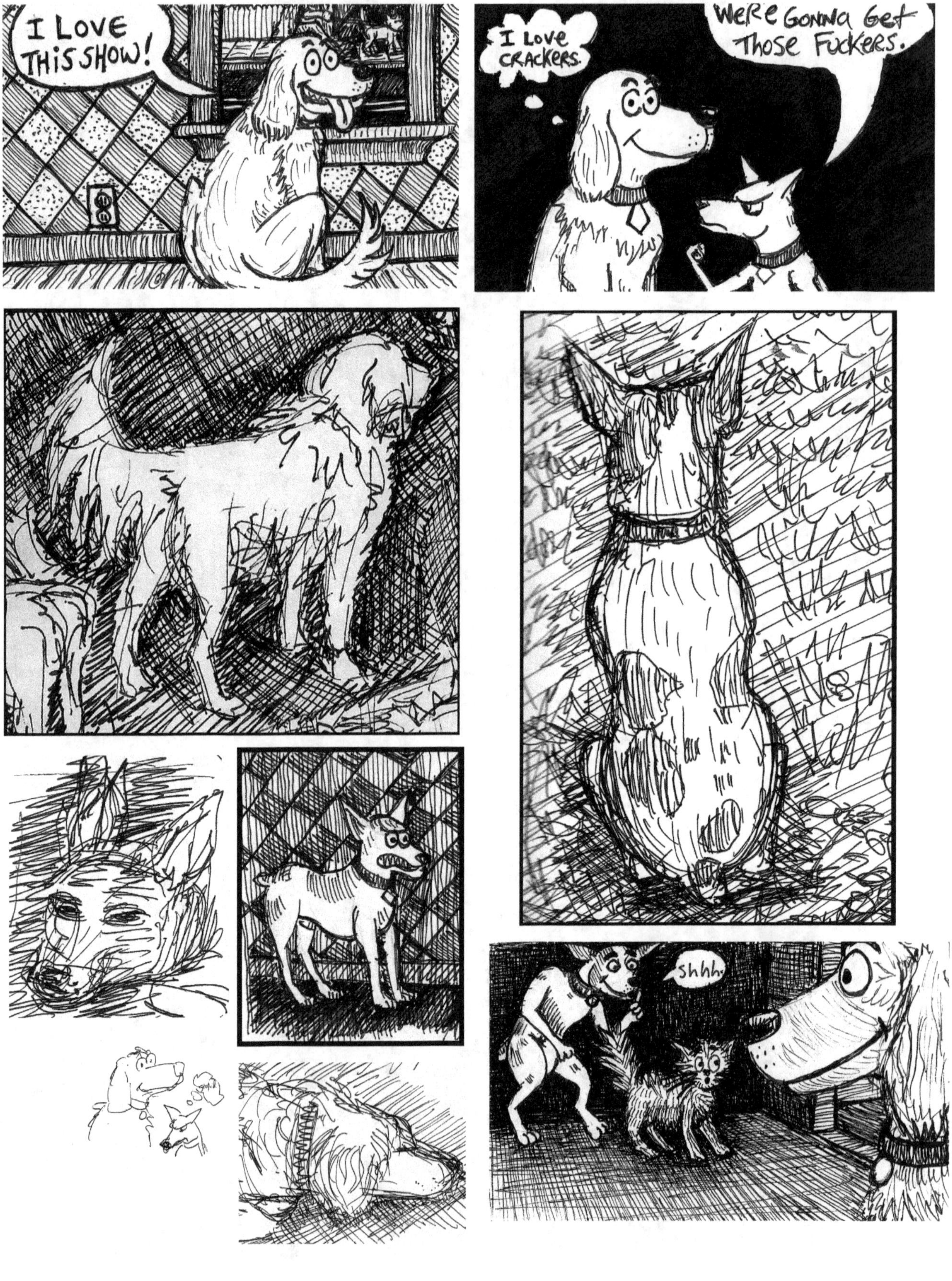

I LOVE THIS SHOW!

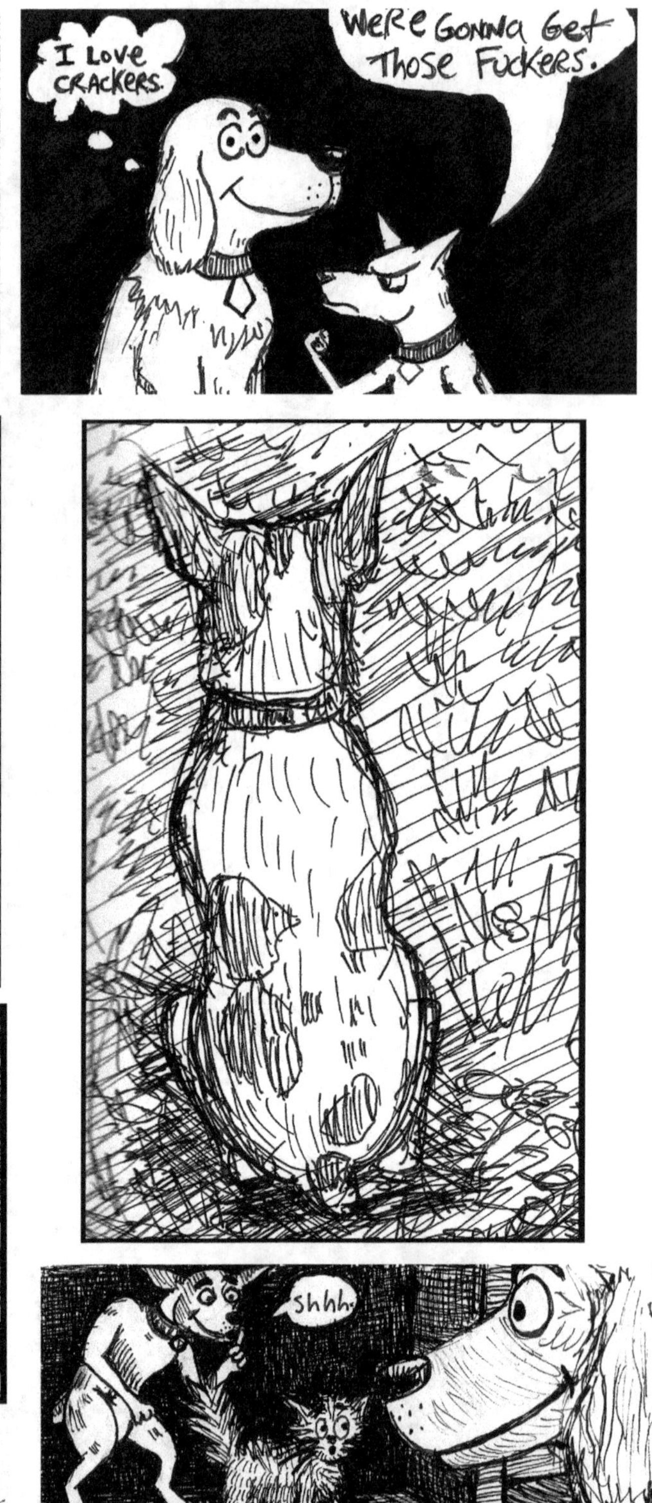

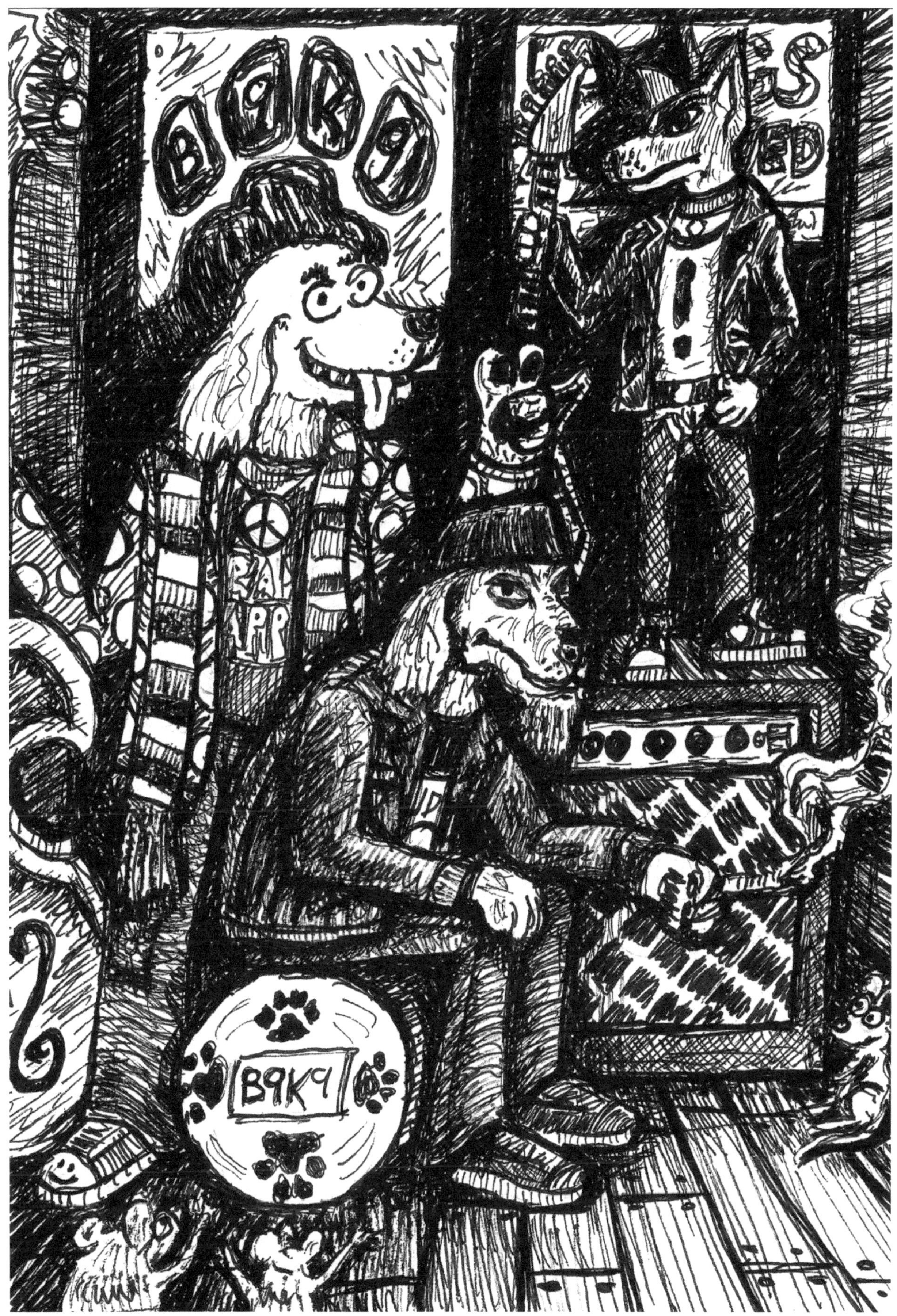
B9K9
B9K9

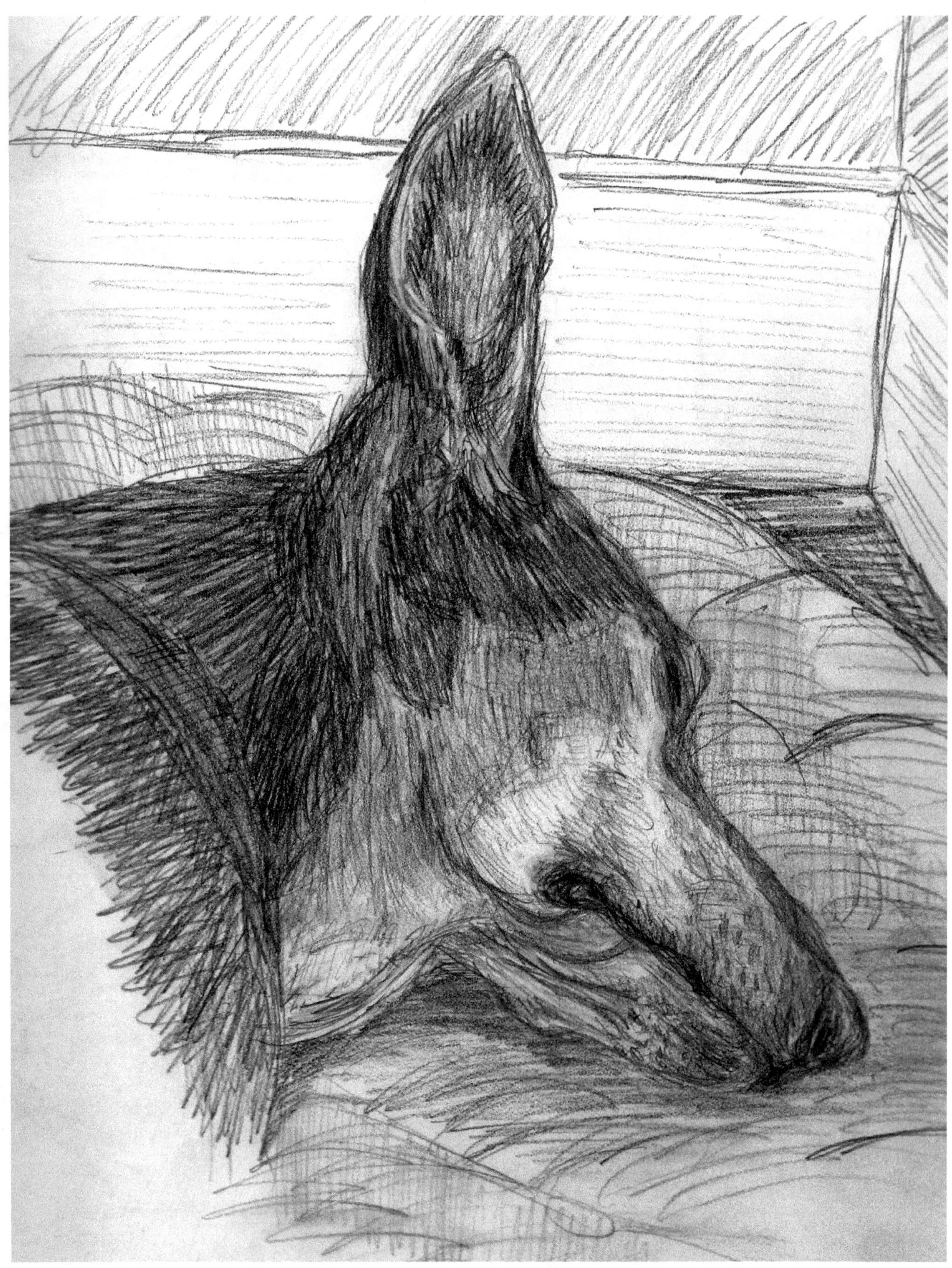

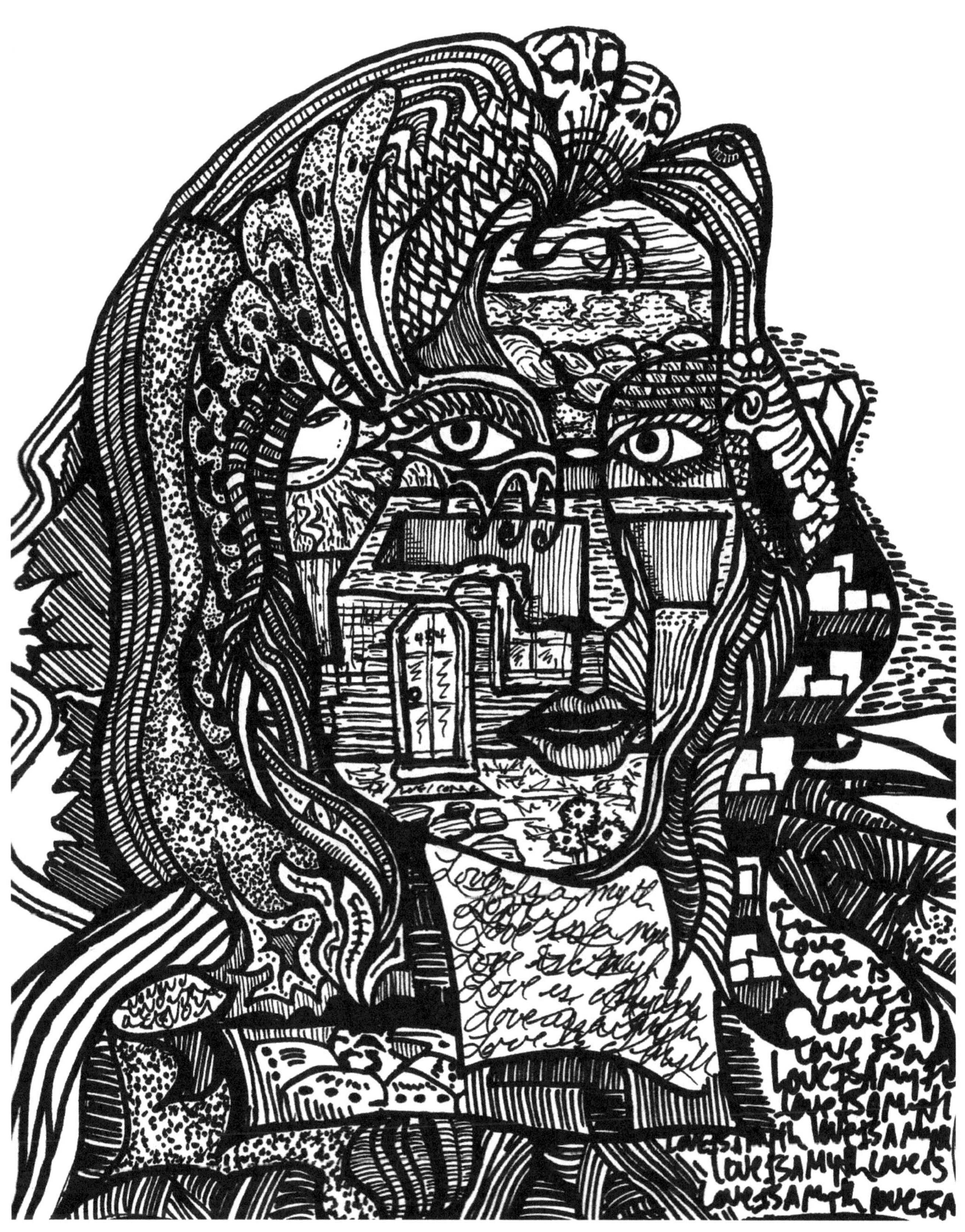

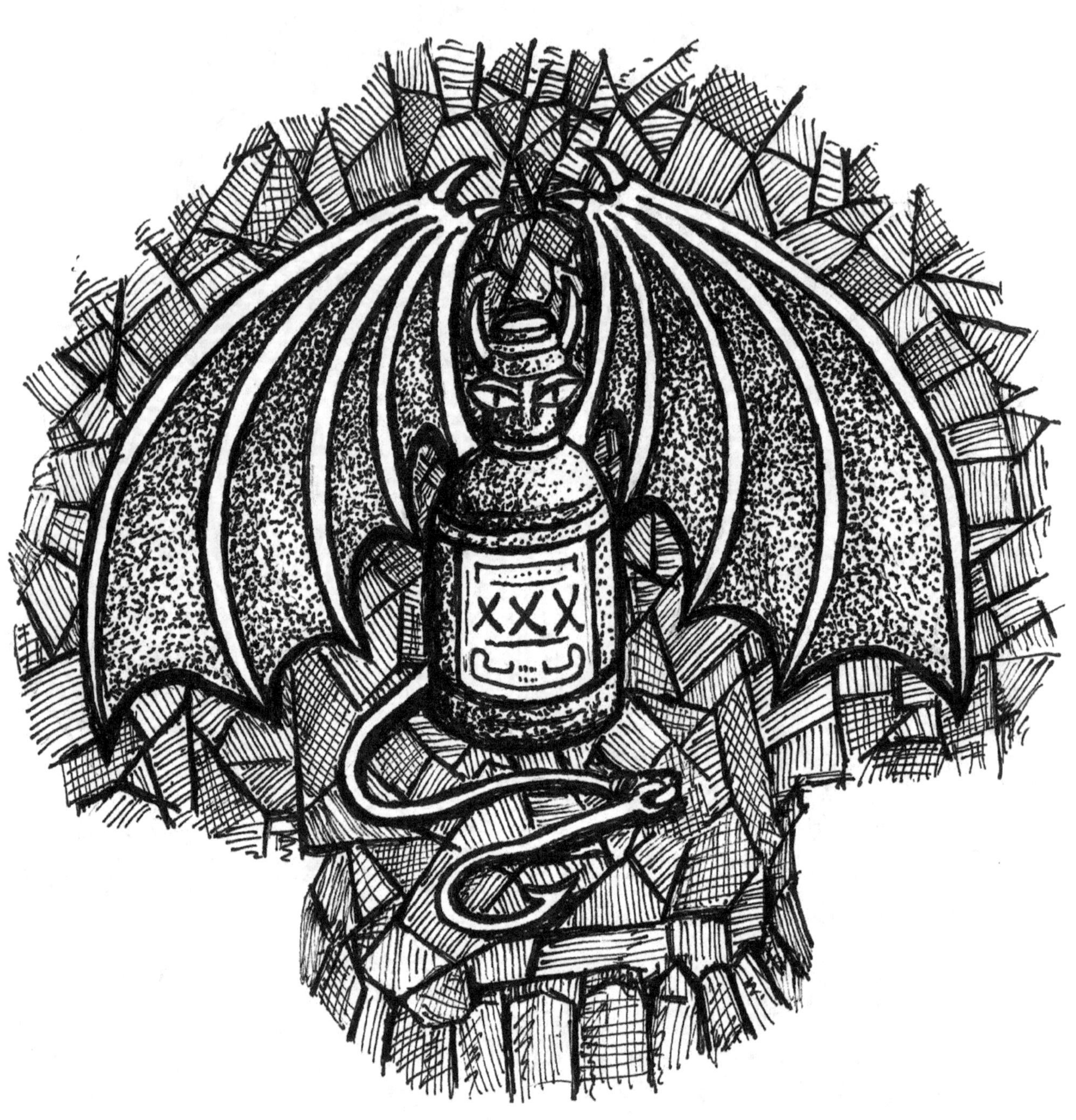
XXX

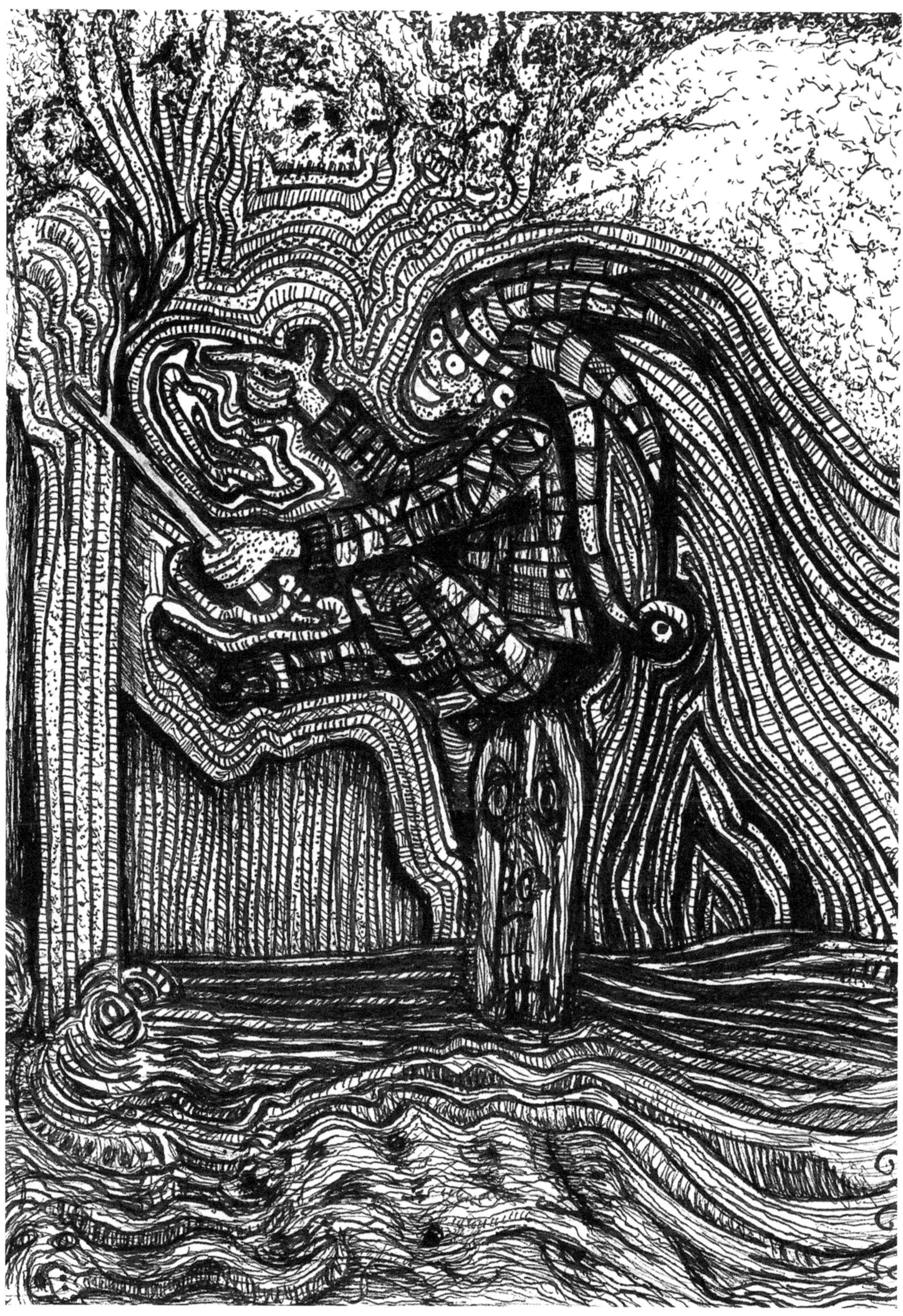

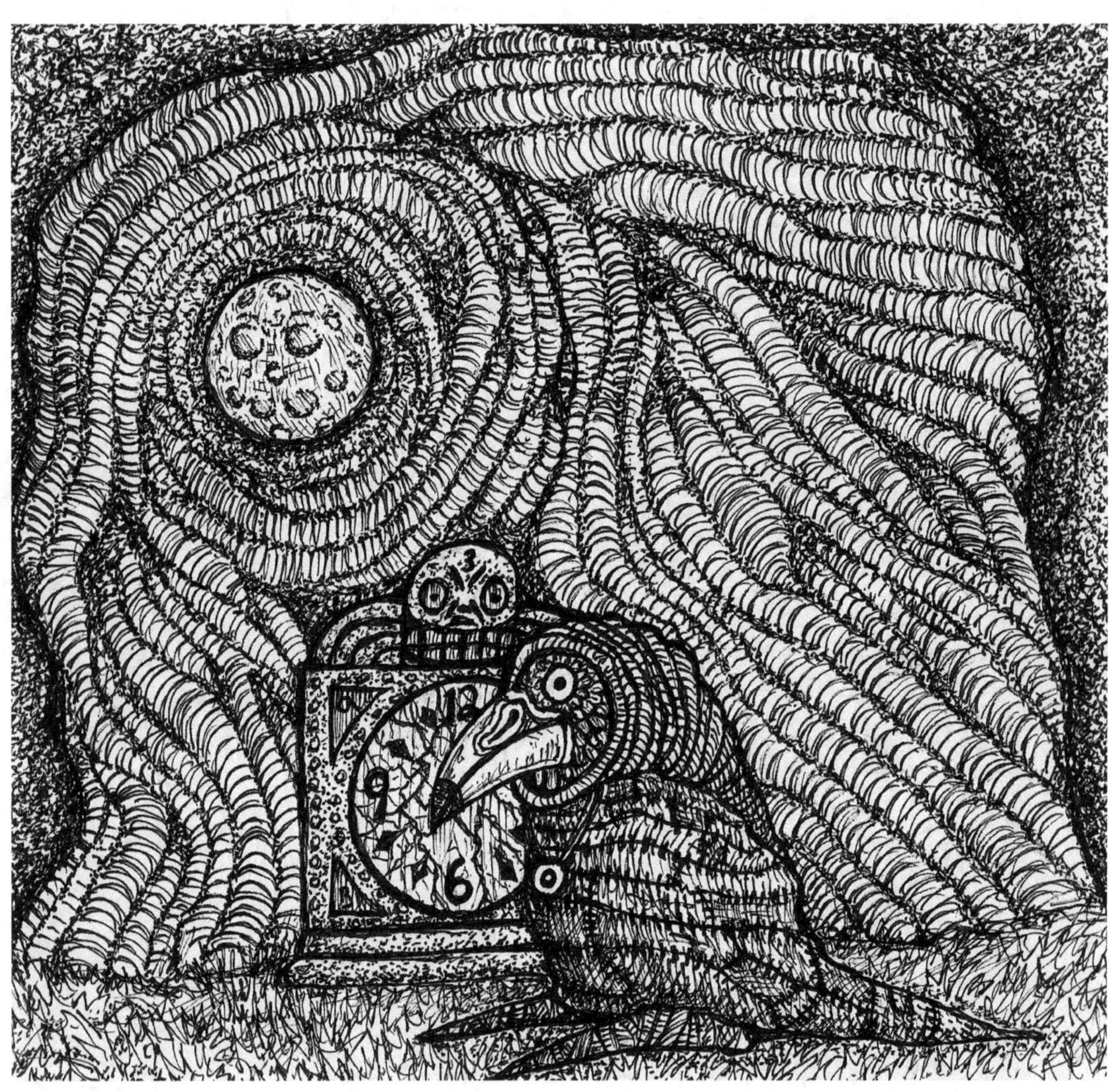

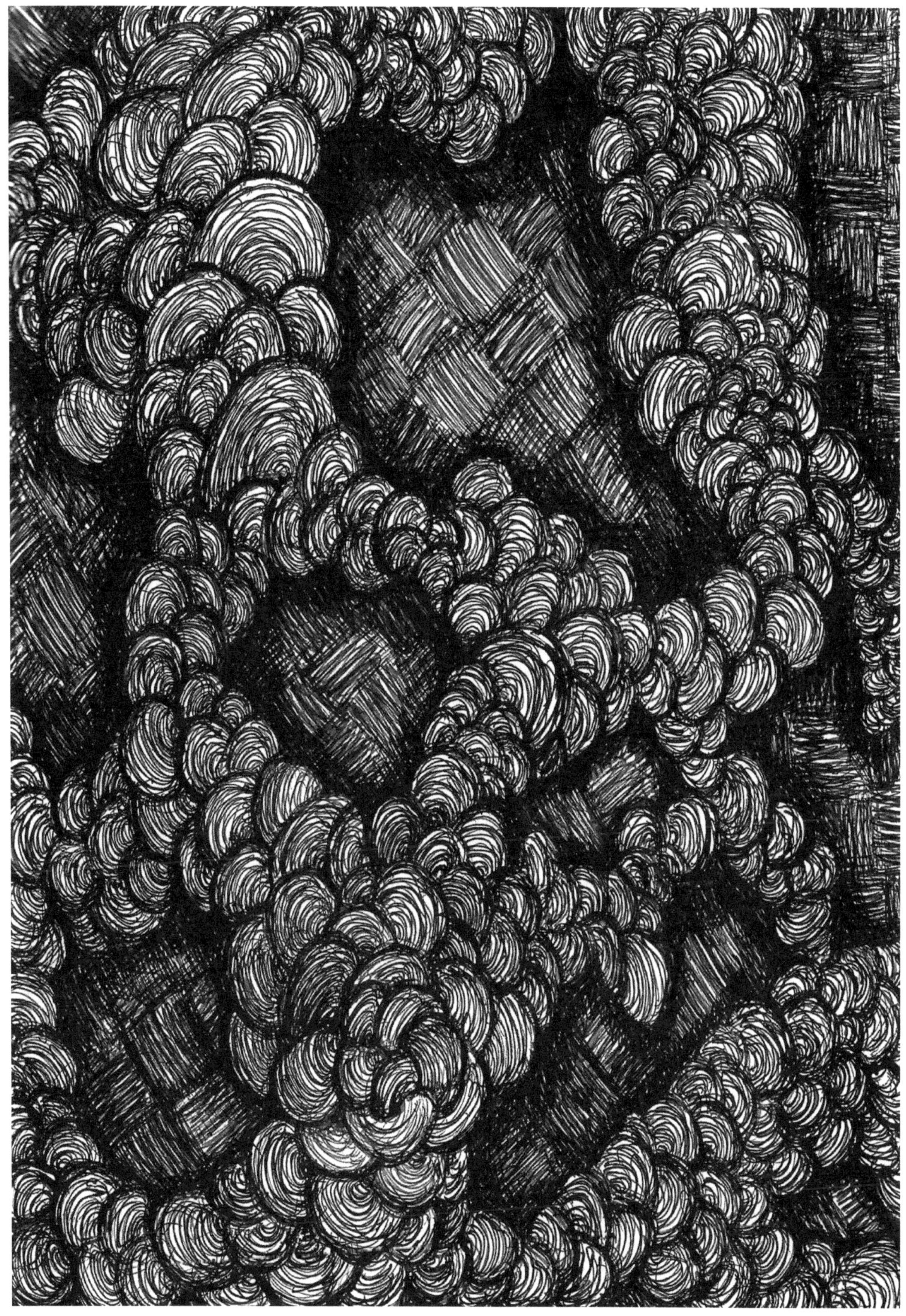

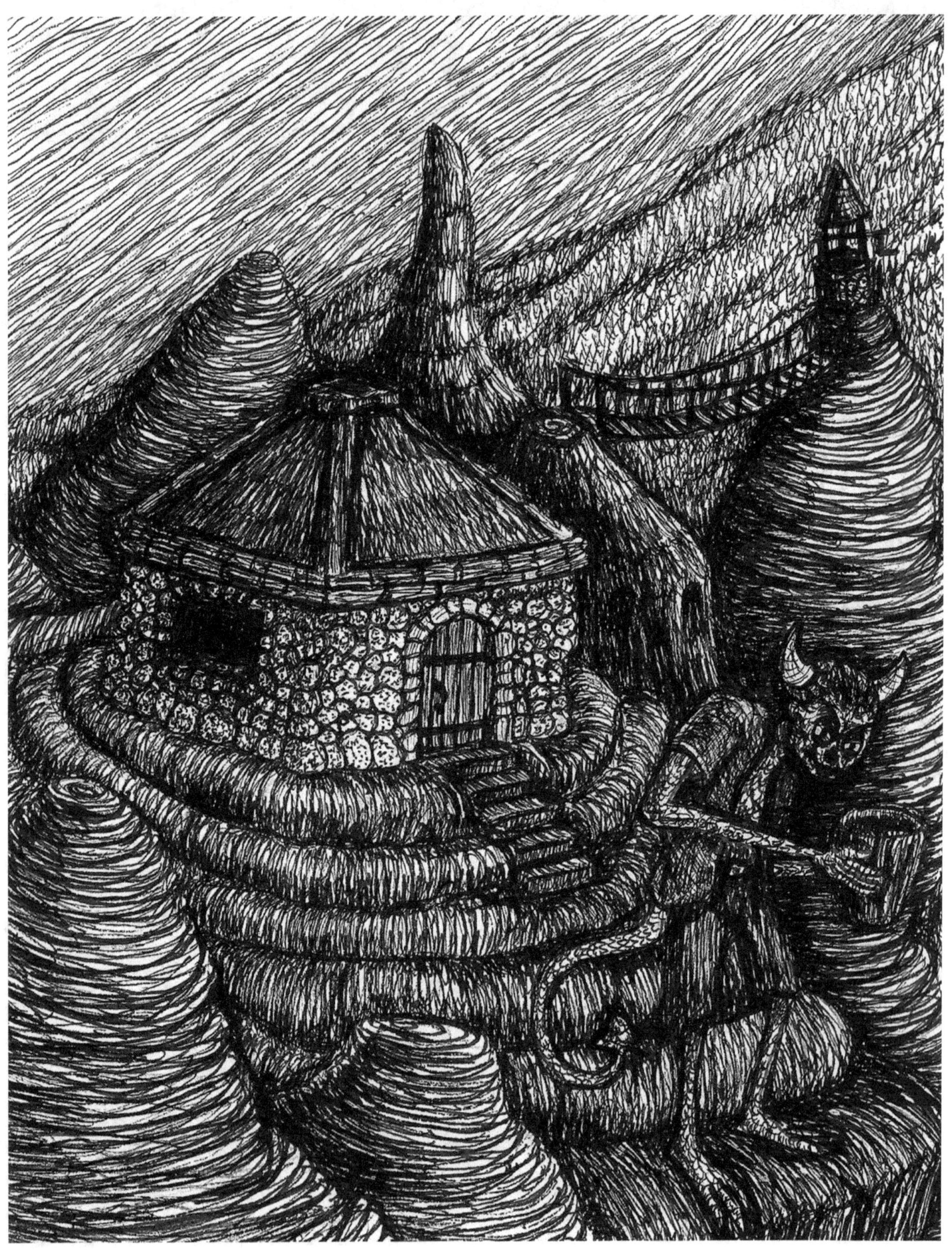

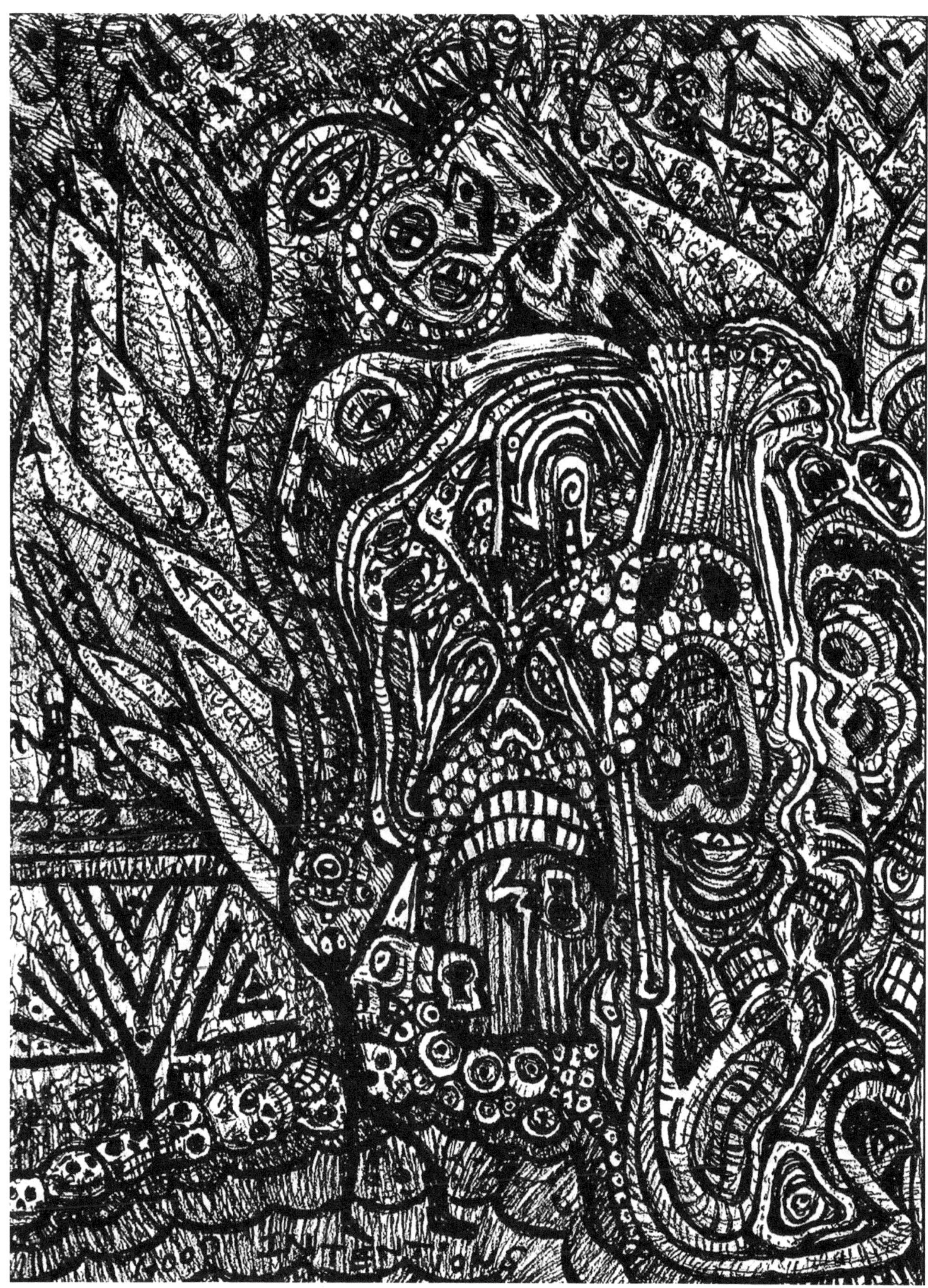

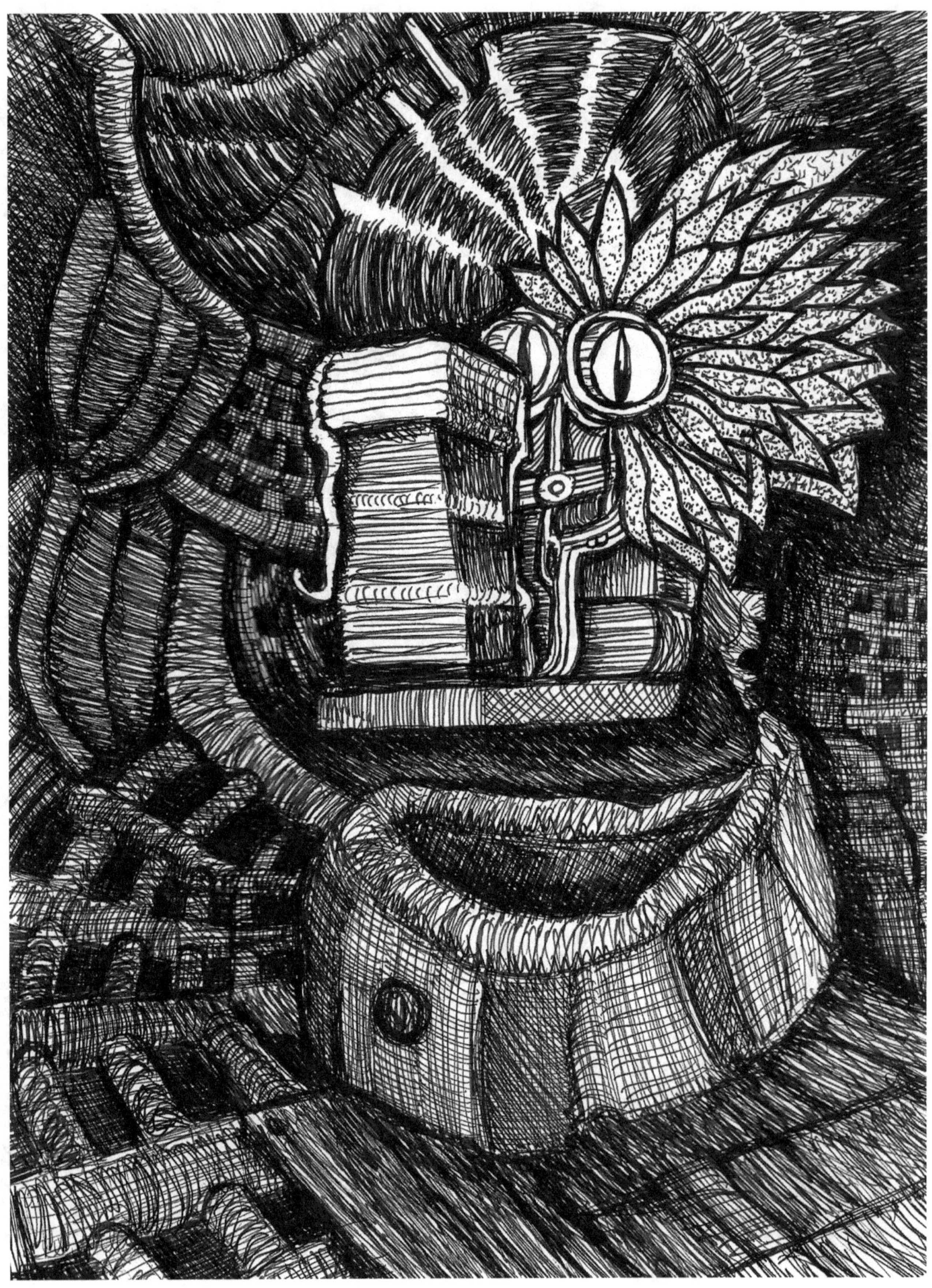

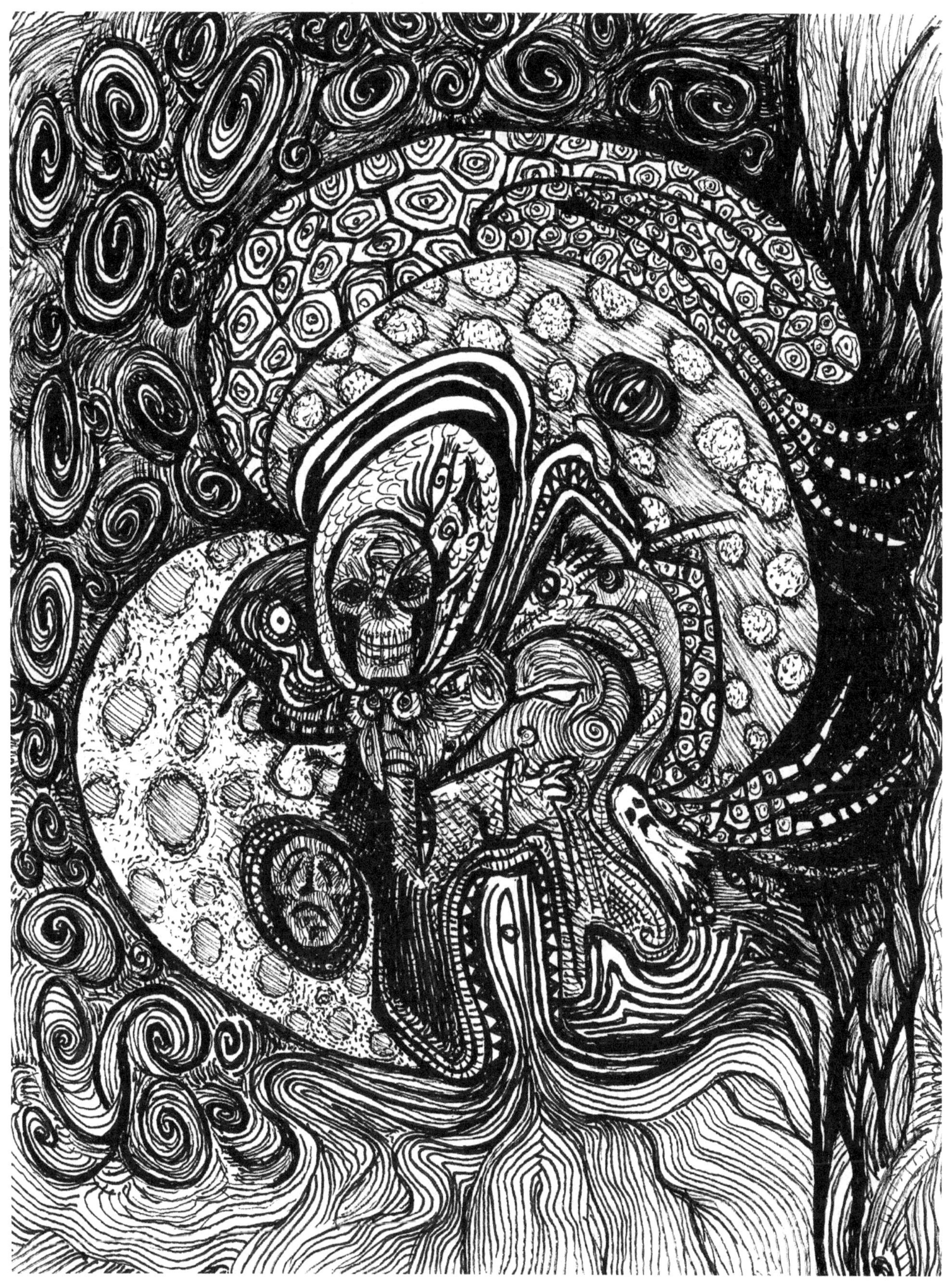

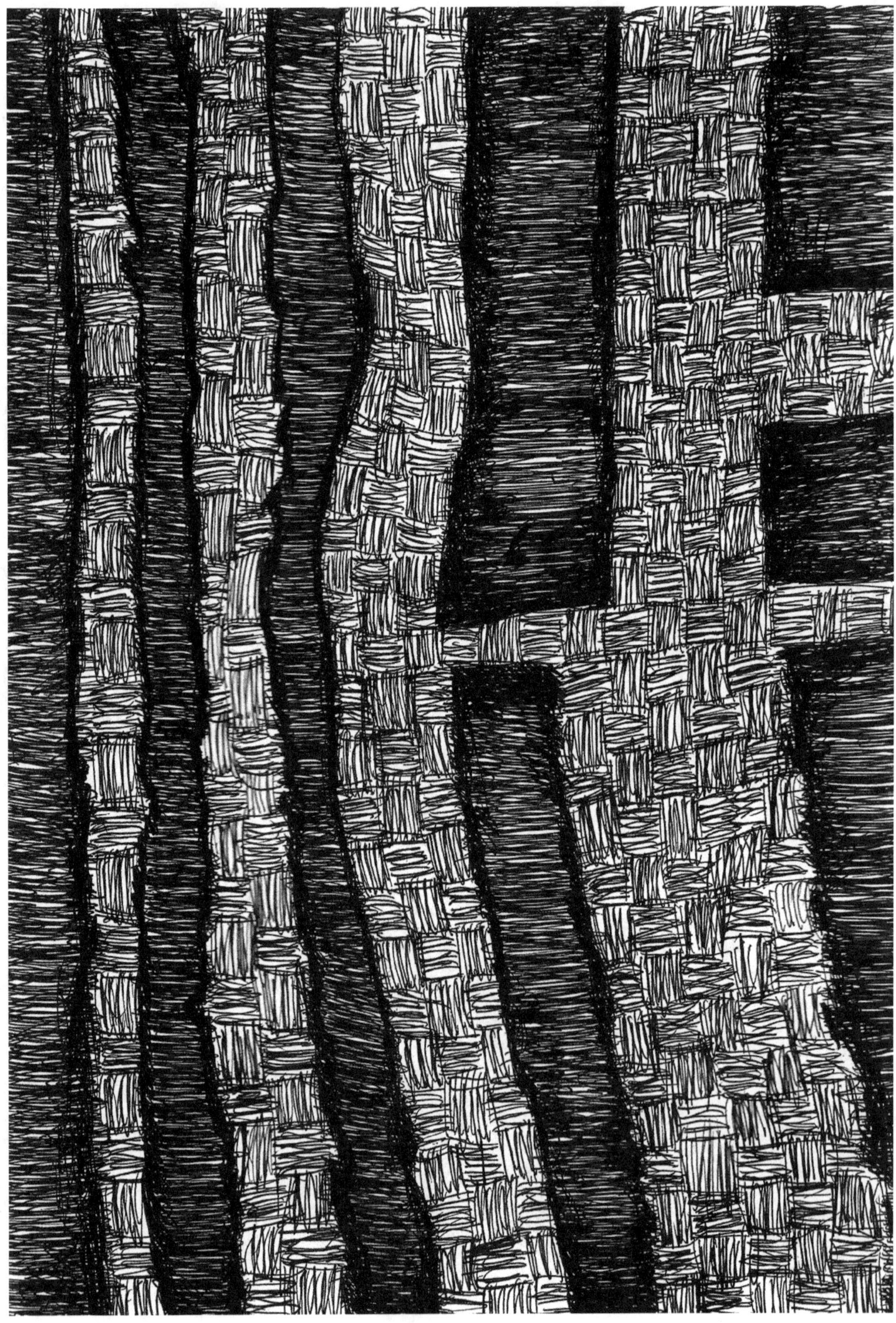

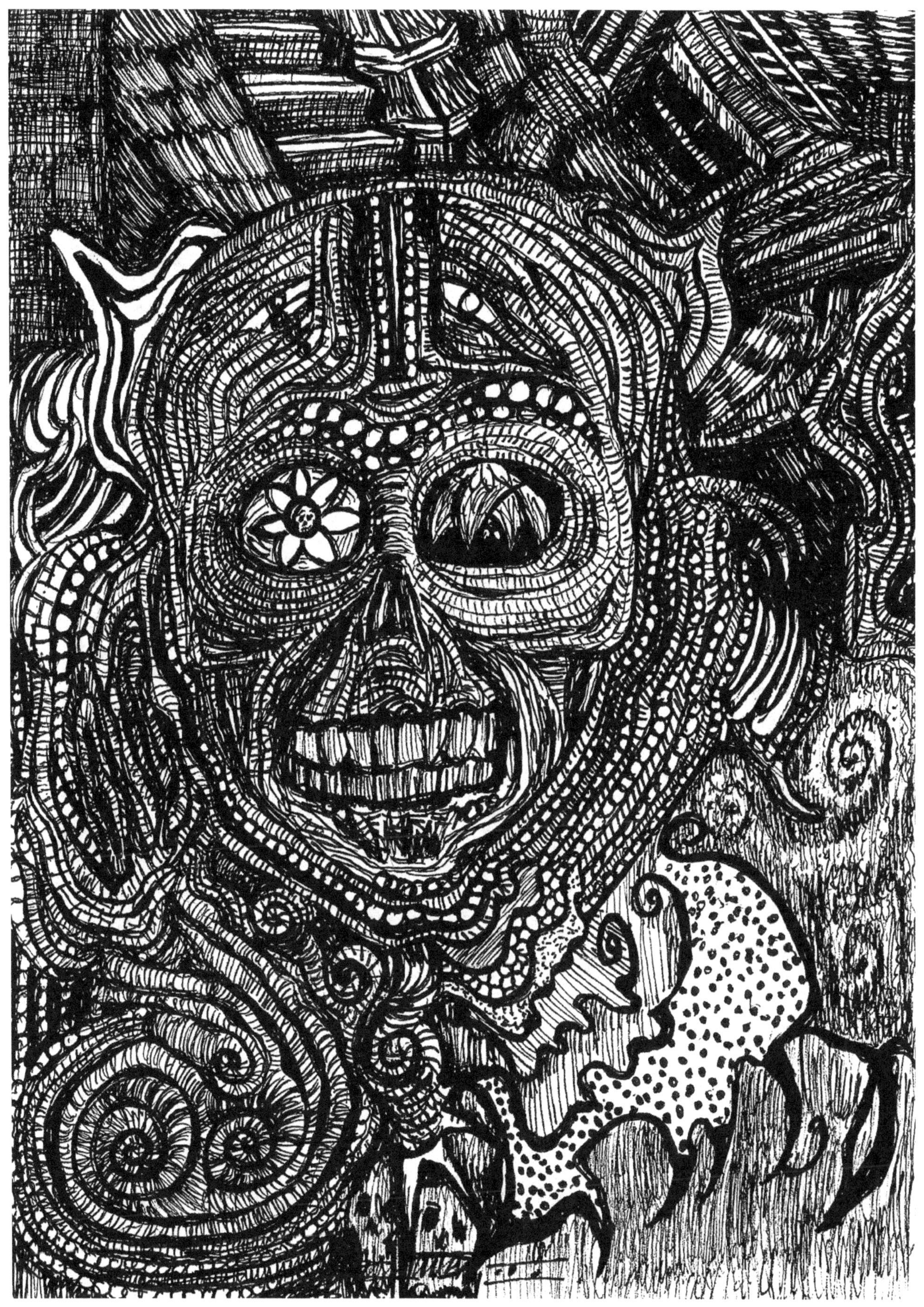

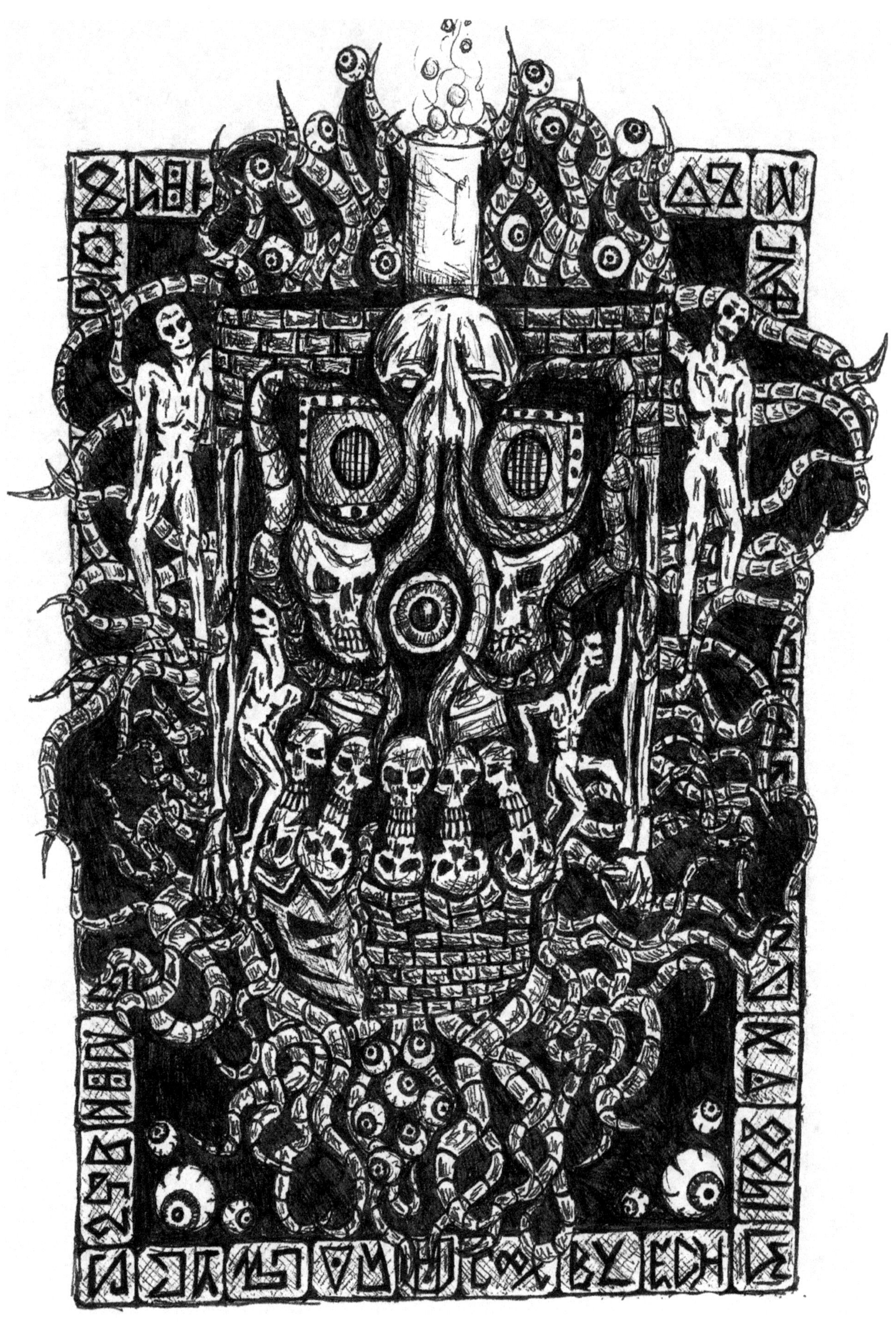

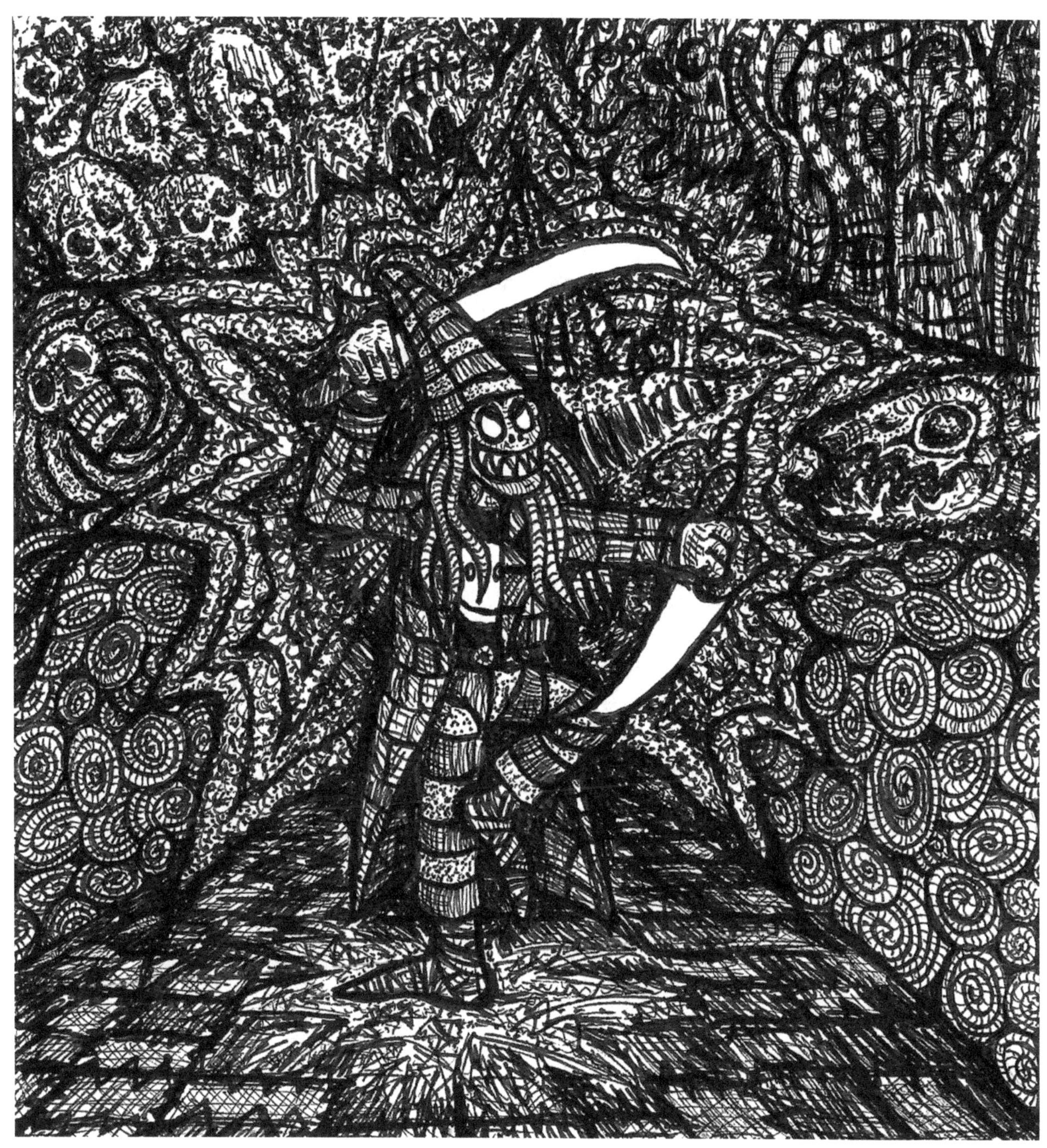

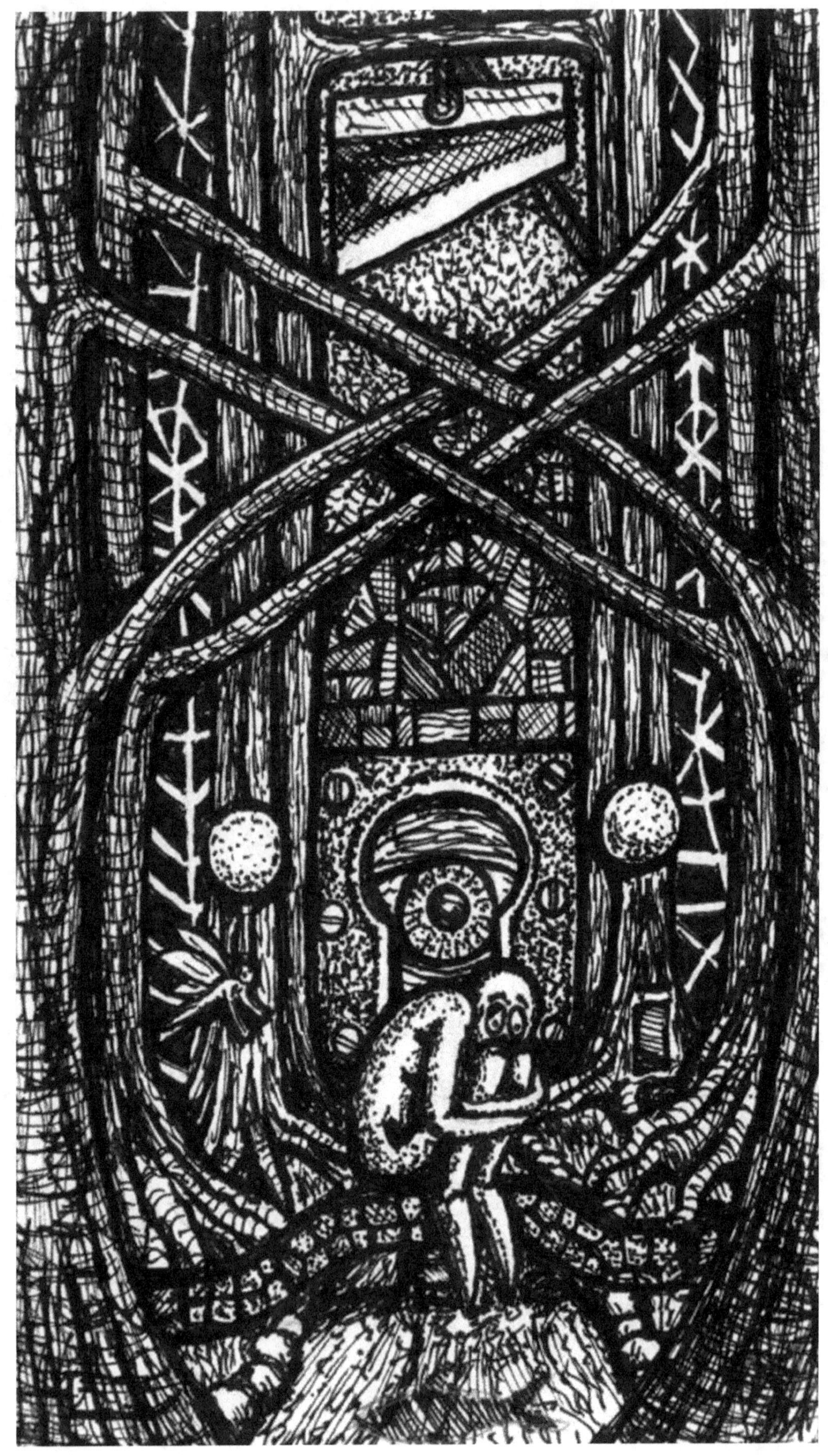

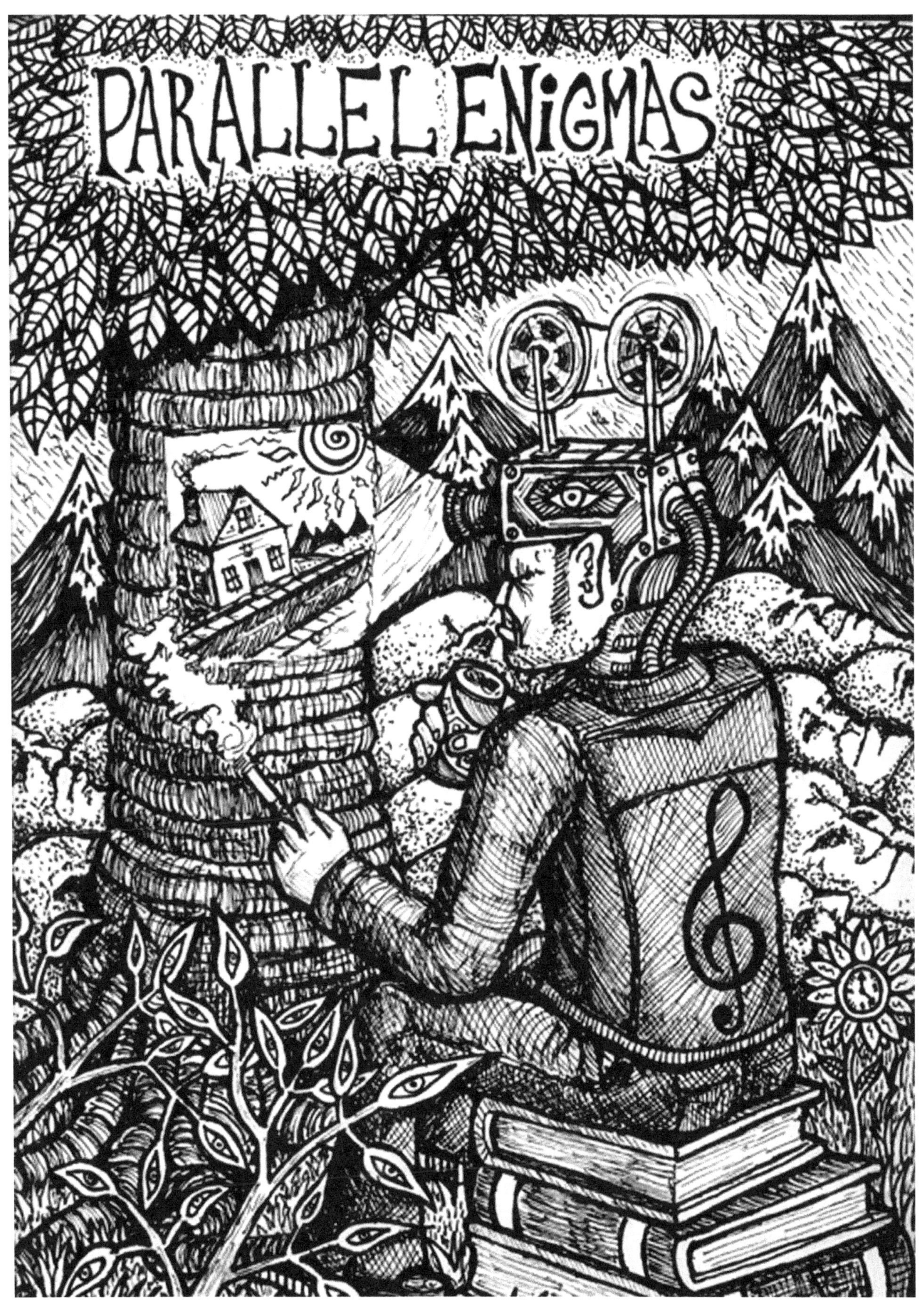
PARALLEL ENIGMAS

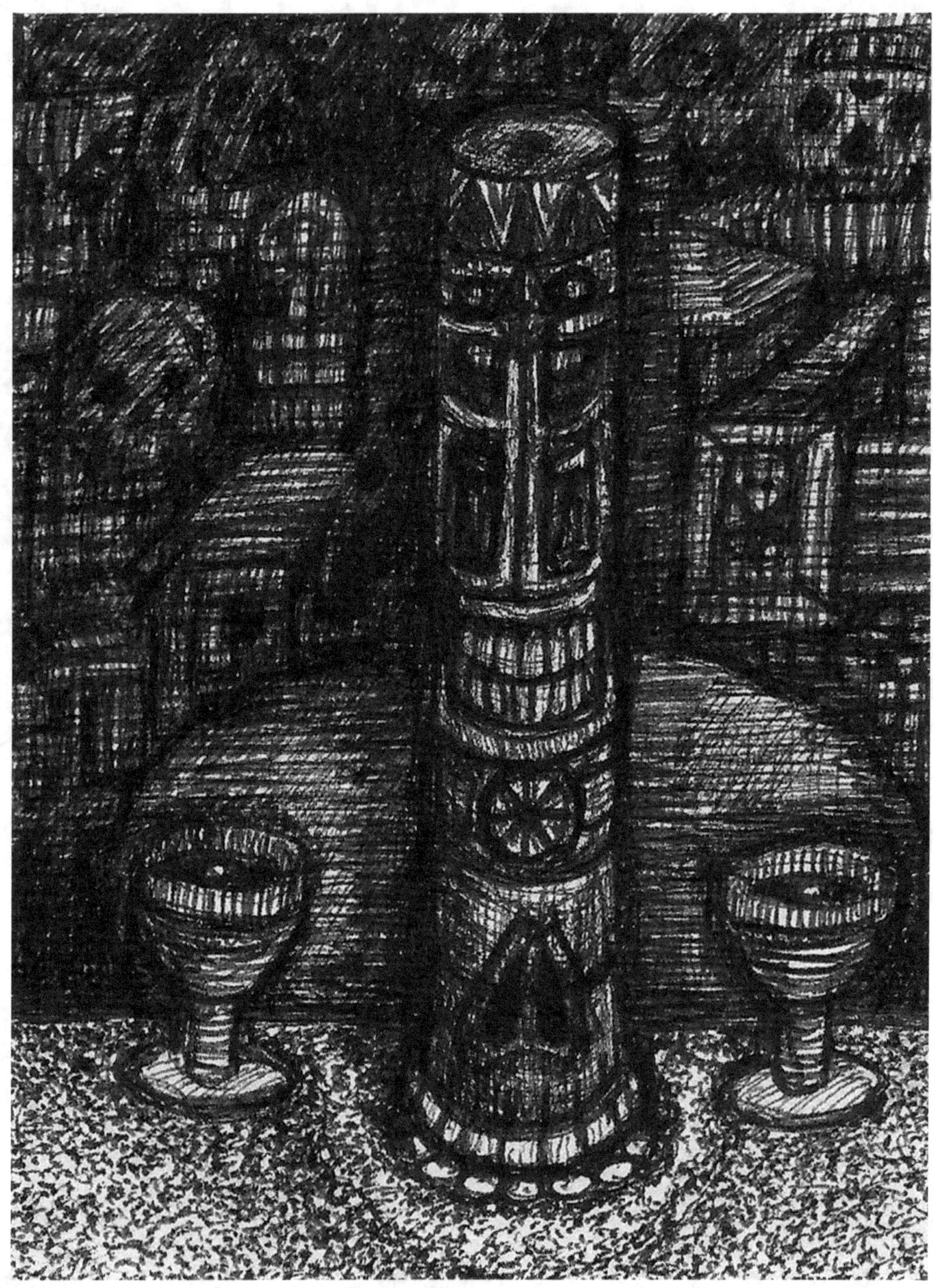

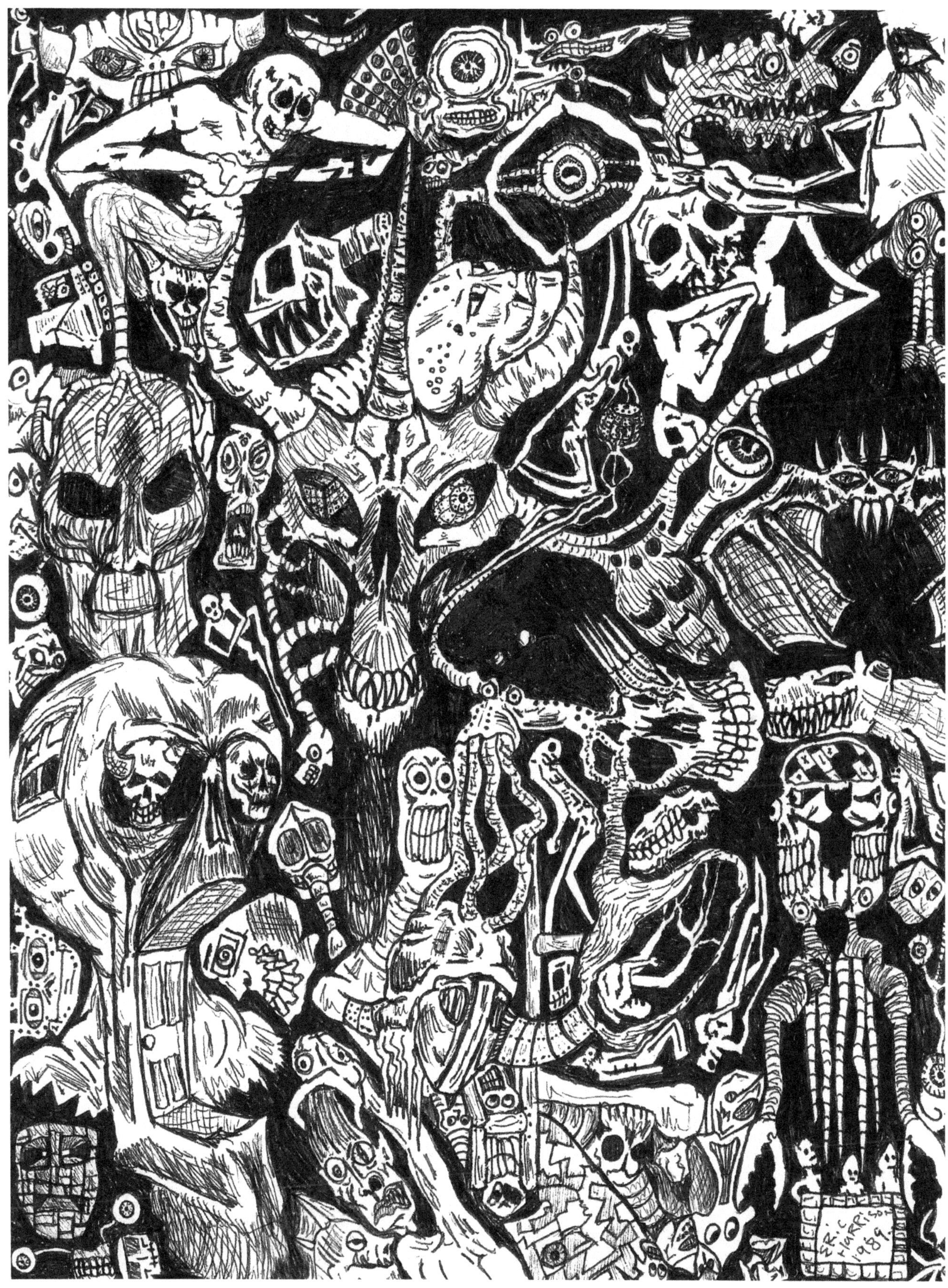
ERiC
HARRiSON
1989.

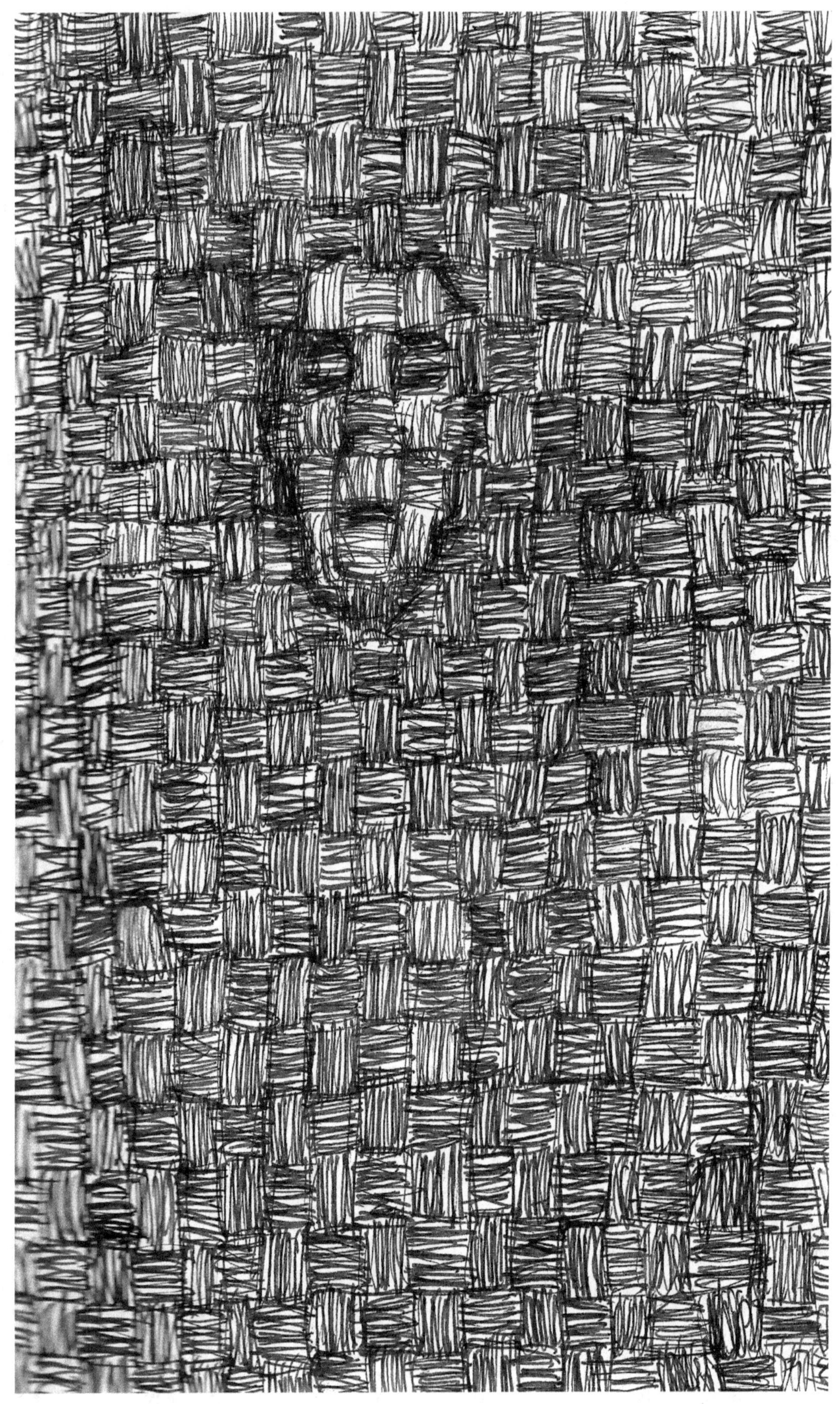

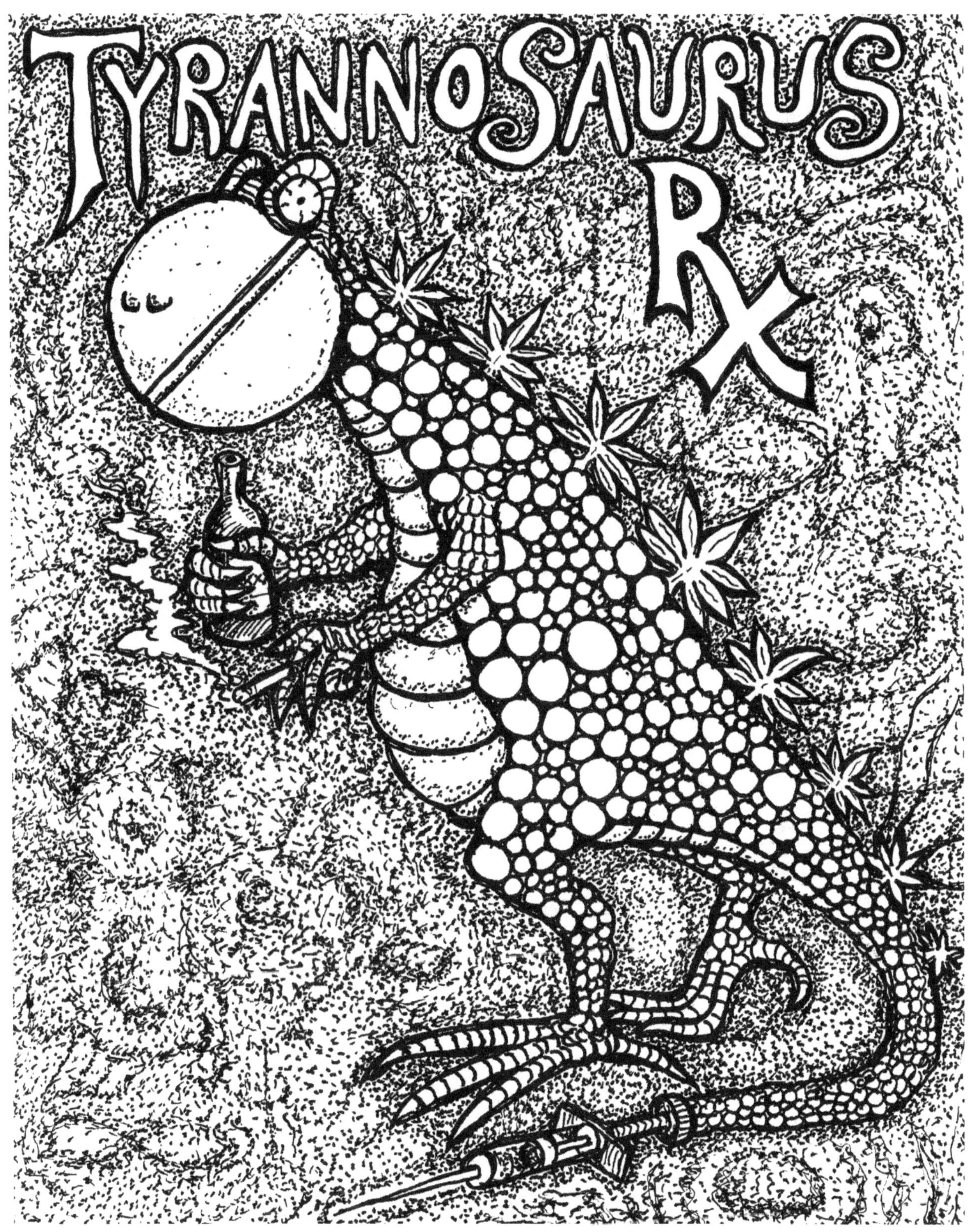
TYRANNOSAURUS
Rx

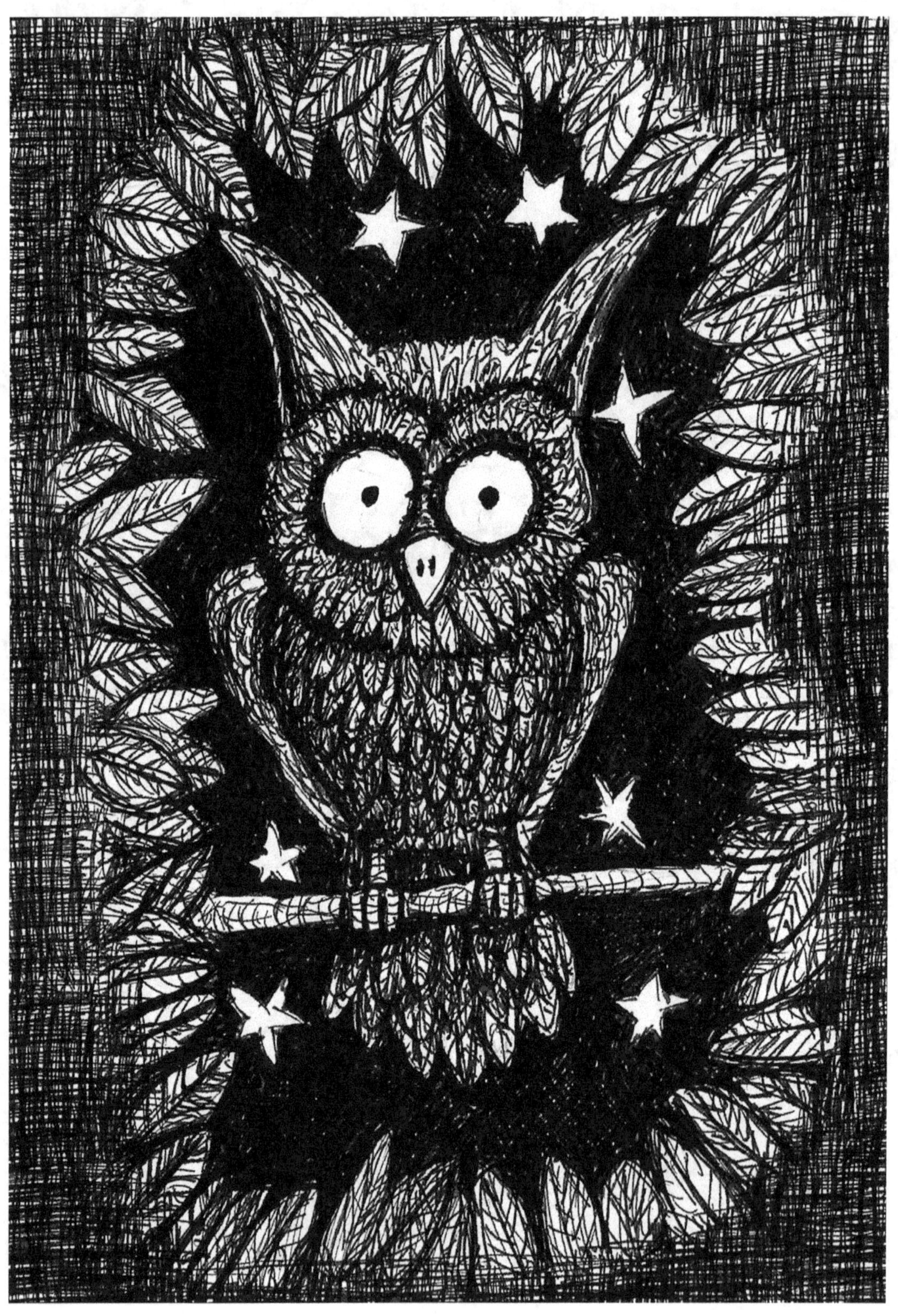

Index / Information about the drawings

SSB is an anagram for "Security Sketch-Book" these drawings were done in transit, in a sketchbook that I carry to reduce anxiety and to control paranoia. They were mostly done on buses and trains or at depots. These SSB drawings are done straight from to paper without any planning or pencil outlines using pigment liners or liquid ink pens; these are raw, unharnessed ideas born straight from me, through the pen to the page. - ech 7/29/2012

3 - "Mouse Voyage" circa 2010. Pigment-liners on paper.

7 -"2 people discuss someone who has died." SSB, Bus Stop, 2011.

9 – "A skull full of death." Pigment liner on paper, circa 2010.

10 - Untitled, SSB Downtown, Salem, Ma, 2011.

11 – "Cthulhu on the rise." Done by a brackish river. Salem, Ma. 2012.

12 –"Dangerous Fish"#1. Pigment-liner on paper. 2005.

13 - "Dangerous Fish"# 2. pigment liner on paper - Saltmarsh Ma. 2005.

14 -"Bird In Teacup"SSB 2012,Salem,Ma

15 – "Apple" Fall 2010. Done after apple picking with my girlfriend.

16 – "Spiral Architecture" – SSB , Beverly MA

17 - Untitled, black liquid ink pen on paper. SSB 2012 – done on a moving bus.

18 – "Doctor Tease." Circa 2004-2005, pen on paper. Used as the back cover art for the live Grief album "Alive" – Southern Lord Records, 2006.

19 – "Doctored Emotions" pigment liner on paper, circa 2005.

20 – "Do Not Feed" – SSB Train Depot, Salem, Ma. SSB, 2012

21 - Untitled – Pigment liner on paper, July 2012. (done in one sitting.)

22 – "Song Geese" - sketched in the marsh, Saltmarsh, Ma. 2012.

23 – "Song Goose" - sketched in the marsh, Saltmarsh, Ma. 2012.

24 – "the brother" - liquid ink on heavy sketch paper. SSB, 2011.

25 - "Murder of Crows"- Psychopomp Series # 5, Pigment liner on paper. 2011

26 - Untitled – liquid ink on sketch paper. SSB 2012.

27 - "Tree of death" – pigment liner on card stock, 2011.

28 - my dogs – pens, pencils, etc. done at different times ...

Index / Information about the drawings

29 - B9K9 (band promo pic.) L to R;, Big D, Eric C. Harrison , Chuck Naked. 2012.

30 - "My Girl, Justice, RIP." Pencil on sketch paper. 2002.

31 - "Actress I Admire" markers on drawing paper, circa 2003.

32 – "Addiction demon" Art for the chapbook "Parallel Enigmas" Third Lung Press (poems by myself & Carter Monroe.) 2003.

33 – "Laughter will save you from drowning" Pigment Liner on paper, 2011.

34 – "Birds keep Secrets" Pigment liner on paper, 2002

35 – "clam clouds" liquid ink on sketch paper, SSB, 2012.

36 – Untitled – pigment liner on paper, circa 2010

37 – "Return To Castle Grief" – original concept sketches for the album "Come To Grief" done in 1995. In 2005 I penned the sketch, expanded upon it. Appears In the 2010 Willowtip Records's rerelease of the LP, Come to Grief.

38 - "In the machine" liquid ink on sketch paper. SSB 2012.

39 - "Beast of Moons" pigment liners on drawing paper, circa 2011.

40 – "Static for Death" liquid ink on paper, SSB 2011.

41 - "Dream Purge:" 2010, drawn on a scrap of paper.

42 - Untitled 1988. This was used for the back of Grief US Tour shirts in 1995

43 - "Battle of The Tatterdemalion" 2005 Art for"Man's Best Friend" picture disk by Noosebomb, Land O' Smiles Records, 2007.

44 - "Waiting" black ink on paper" 1st appeared in The Underbeat Journal # 2, 2003 and was used for T-shirt designs by Grief for the 2008 European Tour.

45 – "Parallel enigmas" – chapbook cover, pigment liner on paper, 2002.

46 - "Sentient place of pagan worship" – black pen on paper, circa 1986-87.

47 – "Old sketchbook demons" 1988, used as interior album art for the LP "brainfood for the braindead", Noosebomb. Shifty Records, 2004.

48 – Face from The Secret Sea – a drawing from the book "Finding the Secret Sea" a book that includes sketches by myself and words by Mike Maguire.

49 –"Tyrannosaurus Rx" Pigment liner on paper. This was a chapbook of collected poems by myself and several other writers, Muertos & Pestle Press. 2004

50 – "Owl" Liquid ink pen on heavy sketch paper, 2012 .

Eric C. Harrison is an American artist, musician & writer of international renown. He works a full-time job and lives a fairly reclusive life in a parallel universe that he calls Saltmarsh with a mermaid, a cat and two dogs. He is often approached by wild animals.

His artwork has been used as album covers and t-shirt designs by numerous underground bands including Abscess, Grief, Noosebomb, Fistula, Stasis, B9K9, -(16)-, Godstomper, No Comply, Chicken Chest and The Bird-boys, Derailer, Esoteric and others. Some of these album covers have appeared alongside record reviews in magazines such as Terrorizer and Metal Maniacs.

His art, poems and short stories have been published sporadically over the years in numerous small-press literary zines and magazines both online and in print including: Tim Peeler's Third Lung Review, Jim Chandler's Thunder Sandwich, The Underbeat Journal, Load of Noise (England,) Mass Movement Zine (Wales) and Boue Magazine (France.)

As a musician Eric is best known for having played bass and doing back-up vocals for GRIEF, a Boston based doom-metal band with a world-wide cult-following. He has played on a number of CD's and vinyl albums and has performed live all over The United States and Europe.

His current music project, B9K9 can be heard on THE WILL TO FAIL compilation CD released by Goat Skull Records in 2013.

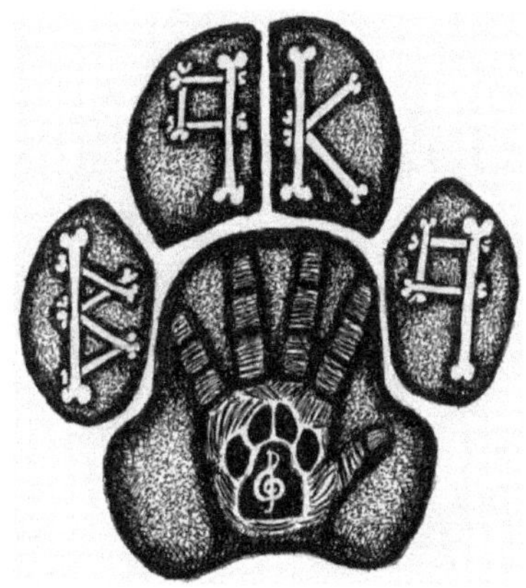

www.ericcharrison.com

www.B9K9music.com

www.facebook.com/ericcharrisonart

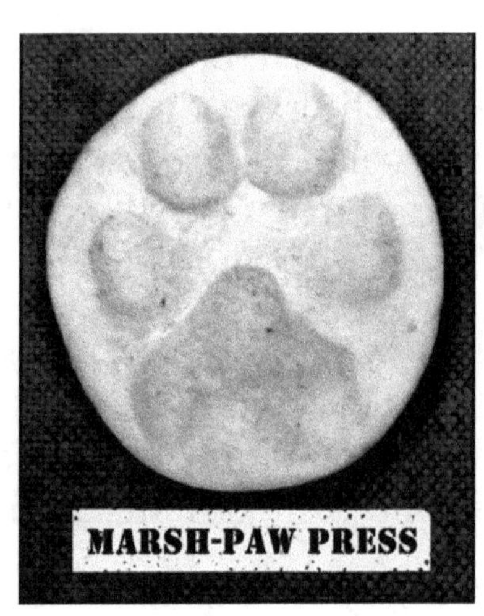

www.marshpawpress.com

www.facebook.com/marshpawpress

www.ingramcontent.com/pod-product-compliance
Lightning Source LLC
LaVergne TN
LVHW080929120826
845149LV00018B/1851
9780988804050